Praise for *How to Read a Client from Across the Room*

"*Knowing oneself is important. However, in sales and business, it's vitally important to know and understand the other person. While doing so in detail is a process, this excellent book provides a method for grasping another's essence quickly and powerfully. Follow the author's advice and you'll find yourself able to touch the lives of many, many more people with the exceptional value of your product or service. The bonus is that not only will your business relationships improve, those in your personal life will, as well.*"

Bob Burg, national bestselling coauthor of
The Go-Giver and author of *Endless Referrals*

"*Powerful, practical, and solid advice on how to read people in any situation. Apply Mychals's knowledge and you'll feel much more confident and ready to rock every potential client opportunity.*"

Dr. Joe Vitale, bestselling author of
The Attractor Factor and *Attract Money Now*
and costar of the hit movie *The Secret*

"*This book unlocks the secrets of connecting to and persuading more people, more quickly. In today's fast-paced world, a book like this is pure gold.*"

Robert G. Allen, author of *New York Times* bestsellers
Creating Wealth and *The One Minute Millionaire*
and many other bestselling books

"*An intriguing blend of business 'how-to,' scientific research, intuitive observation, and pop culture mixed into one unique system that will forever change how you view the world.*"

Janet Bray Attwood, *New York Times*
bestselling author of *The Passion Test*

"*If you'd like to connect with new clients quickly and effectively, you can learn the secrets in* How to Read a Client from Across the Room. *This book offers a powerful guide to attracting new business.*"

Marci Shimoff, *New York Times* bestselling author of *Happy for No
Reason* and *Chicken Soup for the Woman's Soul*

"In How to Read a Client from Across the Room, *Mychals has unlocked the code and given us access to it in an understandable and practical framework for success. This book will help you learn the art and science of reading and understanding people in ways you never thought possible—and don't need years of schooling to get. Practice her techniques and you will rise to the top of your field in no time."*

Dr. Daniel J. Reidenberg, PsyD, FAPA, BCPC, CRS, CMT,
Executive Director of SAVEChair; Advisory Board,
American Psychotherapy Association

"Don't sweat the small stuff when it comes to attracting clients. Success doesn't have to be a struggle, and Mychals new book is paving the way to finding your ideal clients fast."

Kristine Carlson, international bestselling author,
leading expert on success, and author of the
Don't Sweat the Small Stuff series
with her late husband, Dr. Richard Carlson

"Aim high in your business to manifest your greatness and that of your clients. Brandy will provide you the insight and winning strategies to enable you to attract the right clients. Take action now and buy this book to build the business of your dreams."

Les Brown, bestselling author and motivational speaker

"This book is a road map for success in building mutually rewarding business relationships. Use it as a manual for understanding who your ideal clients really are, what drives them, and how to attract them and keep them for life."

Jill Lublin, three-time bestselling author of
Guerrilla Publicity and international speaker

"As CEO of one of the largest women's networking organizations in North America and a multi-million dollar business owner, I know that women want to do more than just 'close the deal.' In addition to providing value with their products or services, women also want to connect on a deeper level and contribute to the world on a larger scale. This is a book that honors all of these desires, allowing you to live a life of success and significance. Brandy Mychals has created a system that

allows you to do this—connect with potential clients, serve their core needs and create lucrative win-win solutions! Without question, this sales book is a must-read for women and men everywhere!"

Sandra Yancey, CEO and cofounder of eWomenNetwork
and bestselling author of *Succeeding in Spite of Everything*

"As one of the nation's foremost fitness and nutrition experts, author, and TV personality, I know how important it is to have incredible people skills—especially in my field of work, helping people overcome weight loss resistance. Mychals's book, How to Read a Client from Across the Room, *will empower every high-performance CEO, entrepreneur, and speaker to up their game and increase their sales."*

JJ Virgin, PhD, CNS, celebrity nutrition and fitness expert,
costar of TLC's *Freaky Eaters*, author of *Six Weeks to Sleeveless & Sexy*,
and President of the National Association of Nutrition Professionals

"Being able to quickly connect with prospects is essential to your success. In this book, Brandy Mychals shows you powerful and practical ways to make that happen."

Jill Konrath, author of *SNAP Selling* and *Selling to Big Companies*

"The Queen of Sales Conversion gives two thumbs up to this comprehensive, fun, and amazingly insightful book about what makes people behave the way they do. Get ready to read a book that will strengthen every one of your relationships and help you be more effective in your sales efforts!"

Lisa Sasevich, bestselling author and creator of the
Invisible Close Sales System

"Brandy Mychals has come up with the hottest, brightest, and most timely 'people' code for the next generation. The Character Code System is chock full of penetrating insights and stellar relevancy for understanding the people you live with, work with, and love. Backed by years of solid research, but packaged in a down-to-earth and humanly accessible language system, I predict this system will be the next BIG thing in understanding relationships. If you want to understand yourself and your world, this is the woman to study with."

Gary D. Salyer, PhD relationships expert

"We all know that first impressions are key in our daily professional and personal interactions. Brandy Mychals' Character Code System provides new and significant tools that will help all of us 'read' each other's behaviors to build greater mutual understanding—major pluses in areas such as leadership development and career services in higher education. I look forward to incorporating her system into the training of my campus activities student event programmers."

Scott Drummond, Associate Director of Campus Life/Director, Campus Activities, Central Washington University

"The Character Code System is a perfect common sense tool with universal application. As an advocate for victims, it is vital to meet our clients where they are emotionally in order to help them without hurting them more. In the midst of crisis, timing is everything, and having the Character Code allows for a quick and effective assessment of the clients' personalities, which will then allow a more meaningful and appropriate response to their needs."

Jennifer Storm, Executive Director of the Victim/Witness Assistance Program in Harrisburg, Pennsylvania, and author of critically claimed books on victim's rights

"An important book offering an innovative approach to assessing your clients' motivations and incentives. A new model of analysis that is a must-read for anyone looking to improve their businesses or their lives."

Margaret Hines, Director, Investor Relations, Alignment Financial Services

"I have learned so much from Brandy and her Character Codes! These codes are like a secret 'tell-all' that help you understand each person you meet and how they need for you to interact! As the CEO of Fitlogic, championing fit standards for women's apparel, I need to know how to talk to potential clients, investors, and high-end joint venture partners. This skill is crucial in my skyrocketing business, and the Character Code System has helped me make those connections quickly!"

Cricket Lee, CEO Fitlogic® and visionary marketer

How to Read
a **Client** from
Across the Room

How to Read
a Client from
Across the Room

BRANDY MYCHALS

New York Chicago San Francisco Lisbon London Madrid Mexico City
Milan New Delhi San Juan Seoul Singapore Sydney Toronto

1 2 3 4 5 6 7 8 9 10   QFR/QFR   1 8 7 6 5 4 3 2

ISBN 978-0-07-180353-3
MHID 0-07-180353-X

e-ISBN 978-0-07-180354-0
e-MHID 0-07-180354-8

Library of Congress Cataloging-in-Publication Data

Mychals, Brandy.
 How to read a client from across the room : win more business with the proven character code system to decode verbal and nonverbal communication / by Brandy Mychals.
     p. cm.
 ISBN 978-0-07-180353-3 (alk. paper) -- ISBN 0-07-180353-X (alk. paper) 1. Personality. 2. Interpersonal communication. 3. Nonverbal communication. 4. Success in business. I. Title.
 BF698.M93 2013
 153.6--dc23

                                                                    2012035357

McGraw-Hill books are available at special quantity discounts to use as premiums and sales promotions or for use in corporate training programs. To contact a representative, please e-mail us at bulksales@mcgraw-hill.com.

For my daughter, Bella,
you are the light of my life!

The ability to have your message land and speak to individuals in their language is the secret behind great love, effective marketing, and outrageous sales.

—Brandy Mychals

Contents

Preface

There is nothing wrong with you—or anyone else.

That's the bottom line to the Character Code System. As you read this book, you'll discover how this revolutionary system is changing the way we conduct business, marketing, speaking, and sales. You'll see the implications for your personal life as well as for your relationships, health, parenting, and lifestyle.

When all is said and done, you will be totally clear on who you are, what your strengths are, what your challenges are, and why you do what you do.

You'll understand your prospects, clients, coworkers, family, and friends. This book will forever change how you view yourself and the world around you.

You will never look at someone the same way again.

Buckle your seatbelt; it's going to be a wild ride!

How to Read
a **Client** from
Across the Room

Introduction

My Story of Transformation

The journey to create something new, bold, and brilliant is rarely an idea that you just wake up with one morning. It often develops as a result of a lifetime of learning, struggle, and transformation. If we're lucky, we are able to take that moment of transformation and use it to change our lives and chart a new direction. This is the story of my wild ride—with a few crashes along the way—in creating the Character Code® System.

My journey began with a promising career in communications as I earned my undergraduate degree from the prestigious Honors College at Loyola Marymount University. My education was diverse, including courses in journalism, English, psychology, behavioral studies, media, and marketing—all the ways we can communicate with those around us. I could have had a career in media, writing, teaching—anything was possible. I was young, idealistic, and invincible. Or so I thought.

Not long before graduating, I was driving down the Pacific Coast Highway on a warm day in Los Angeles. I remember smiling as light came through the sunroof of my bright-blue Honda Civic. My field of vision was clear as I zoomed back toward campus.

Out of nowhere I saw a tire hurtling toward me.

It was so out of the ordinary to see a tire flying through the air that it took a moment to register that I was set on a collision course, and with oncoming LA traffic there was nowhere to go. The full-size tire and rim slammed into the roof of my car, crashed through my sunroof showering me with glass, and hit me on my head before rolling off my car. Shaken, I somehow managed to pull over to the side of the road.

It was a freak accident of a tire falling from the freeway overpass above. The police surmised it was an extra tire that bounced out of the back of a pickup truck, and the driver probably had no idea he lost it until he arrived at his destination minus his cargo. He would wonder what had happened, and meanwhile I was left with a totaled car and significant head trauma.

It took over a year to recover from that injury. I dealt with a lot of body aches and pains along with some memory loss. During the recovery, I embarked on a new journey of healing. This experience led me to Chiropractic College. It was a complete shift of gears and required me to move from the land of language and arts into science and medicine.

For someone who was never that interested in school, I found myself spending a lot of time and money on my graduate education. I brought my communications background with me and worked as a writer and tutor during years of study. I used my behavioral studies in all my interactions with colleagues and patients. I was constantly observing, noting, and learning more.

It took years to earn my doctorate, and I graduated second in my class. I was now married, was building a successful chiropractic practice, and was a mom to a very happy baby girl, Bella. I reinvented our business, bringing in substantial income, invested, and at one point owned eight homes. I had created almost $2 million in wealth in just a few years, and life looked good. I had just been published in a peer-reviewed scientific journal and was in the best physical shape of my life. The story of injury and struggles was far behind me, and I was back on track.

I hopped into my Saab and headed to the Claremont Resort and Spa in Berkeley. Bella was playing at home, and I was sneaking off to exercise for an hour. Traffic was sluggish with everyone headed to San Francisco, and I was trying to be patient with the delays. I could see the frustration on the faces of the other drivers.

I heard the screech of brakes before I felt the impact. It happened so quickly, there was no time to react. A large Mercedes was trying to race into the lane behind me and misjudged the distance. The driver ended up crashing straight into the back of my car. The seatbelt locked, injuring my ribs and shoulder, and my head slammed back against the seat.

My first thought was, "Not again." The driver was very apologetic, assuring me he would repair the car. I had trouble focusing. I remember thinking; *this is the last thing I need.* I didn't care about the car. I was worried about the impact to my body.

The muscle aches from that accident were significant. The pain kept coming on stronger days and weeks after the injury. I tried to work, and it quickly became clear that I would not be able to physically perform as a chiropractor anymore. It hurt just carrying Bella around the house. It was a crushing blow to realize I would not be able to practice. My plans and dreams for the future came to an abrupt halt.

It seemed like that would be enough, but it turned out to be much worse than we expected. After a year of struggle, memory loss, the inability to read, and emotional turmoil, I found myself at Princeton and then Harvard—not as a student but as a medical case. It turned out that the accident had caused several brain lesions. I was diagnosed with a form of epilepsy, migraines, and post-traumatic stress disorder. I was prescribed a handful of daily medications. The brain scans, expert reports, and labels said I would forever be disabled.

The stress was too much for my marriage, and I found myself a young, single mom with a 19-month-old baby. I was unemployable and totally lost. If I had known what the next several years would bring, I probably would have fled—I had no idea of the additional challenges that lay ahead.

I focused on raising my daughter and spent many years hiding from the world and creating a cocoon of safety for the two of us. I was unable to read or work. I faced contentious legal battles from my ex-husband, and all the wealth that had been created flew out the door to pay attorneys and medical bills. I was on social security disability and had no real future to look forward to.

I was immediately faced with having to take a hard look at myself. I was living every day surrounded by Beanie Babies, finger foods, and crayons. I rolled out of bed in the morning, tossed my hair in a ponytail, and pulled on my gray sweatshirt with the hole in the left shoulder, my red sweatpants that were two inches too short, and my fuzzy Elmo slippers. I was lucky if I got to take a shower.

In creating my cocoon of safety with my daughter at home, I was hiding from the world. I had real reasons to hide, but the benefits weren't worth the cost. I was scared that people would find out that I was injured or that I couldn't read. I was afraid they would know how much I had lost and how hard I had fallen. I was scared they wouldn't like me—but I took that first step anyway.

When my daughter Bella was 4½ years old, I signed up with a direct sales company selling jewelry. I hated direct sales and didn't wear jewelry. However, I was desperate to start making some money, and I didn't want to have to be away from my daughter much.

And the result is that this starter jewelry sales job got me to reenter the world of adults, to speak in complete sentences, and to start to dream of a future again. I began to be creative in more than just preschool arts and crafts projects—I started to invent my own business.

Over the next few years I took one step after another. I used my trusted communication skills to connect with my clients. I studied additional behavioral profiling systems, marketing, networking, and sales training. I still feared sales and began to dissect the differences between marketing a product, a service, and information. My business became my lab for testing how to share information to connect with clients that led to a sale without having to be "salesy."

Along the way I learned a lot about my product. This was a new world for me. I had never cared about fashion, jewelry, makeup, or anything along those lines. I worked with thousands of clients over those years, and I made an interesting discovery—people were showing up in a way that illustrated what their personality was. They didn't even have to be aware of it.

Once I made this connection, I was able to know who they were as soon as they walked in the door. This meant I could now communicate with them in a way they preferred—which led to the best sales results. I knew if they were likely to buy and what they would want to buy. This is when things really started to change.

I rebranded as "Jewelry for Your Target Market" and started speaking, teaching men and women how to identify and communicate with potential clients for better sales results. My business grew, and yet I felt the direct sales model was too confining for the type of business I really wanted to create.

Exactly seven years after the accident with my Saab, I was able to start reading again. I stepped up my business training. I weaned myself off all the medication I had been taking from the car accident. Then I sat down and wrote the Character Code System, combining 20 years of study, research, and observation. I quit my jewelry sales job. I was completely out of funds, and my daughter and I were now living at home with my mom. I had no safety net, no backup plan, and nowhere else to go.

This had to work.

So with zero clients, zero dollars, and zero mailing list, I launched a brand-new business out of my mom's spare bedroom. I used the Character Code System as my marketing and sales guide and just leapt.

Within a few months I had a sold-out consulting practice. Within six months, I had my first six-figure sales month. Within the first year I generated over $300,000 in sales, had 80 speaking dates, and won an international award. I attracted book and TV deals and now live in a beautiful home with a million-dollar view.

Life is very different.

This book is about the system I created, the Character Codes, which launched it all.

ONE

The Creation of the Character Code System

Driving Needs and a Quickstart Guide to Character Coding

A
S HUMANS, WE seek to understand and we desire to be understood. Most often in life, however, we fall short in both categories. What we really want to know is the *why*. Why do we do things the way we do, why do the people around us behave the way they do, and why do they sometimes drive us nuts.

Personality typing is not a new discovery. It has been around for thousands of years; one of the first organized systems was created by Hippocrates. Many have referred to the pioneers in this field as "behaviorists" because they studied and noted patterns in human behavior; it was their work that led to the birth of psychology.

Many systems were introduced in the psychologically inclined twentieth century, such as the Myers-Briggs Type Indicator and the DISC Classic Profile, easily the two best known and most widely used in corporations and university settings.

I have personally spent decades studying and using profiling systems in my business, education, and personal life. They have been immensely helpful. However, I discovered limitations with the existing systems. Most are based on a four-type model and require a test to create a profile. The result: you are an "ISFJ," a "High S," a "Phlegmatic," or an "Otter." The terms often have no meaning, you need an advanced degree to interpret the results, or the classification systems aren't memorable.

Some profiling systems have so many subtypes and letter designations that they are nearly impossible to discuss or use in everyday life. In other words, they aren't *user-friendly*. I also felt that most did not dig deeply enough; they provided a superficial understanding without getting to the real *why*.

So I created a new system of classifying people. This method of Character Coding came from over 20 years of personal study, observation, discovery, and my synthesis of thousands of years of theory and research. Best of all, you'll have it mastered by the end of this book!

Testing is optional rather than required. In our visual and fast-paced twenty-first-century lifestyle, we need to be able to communicate more quickly, understand better, and make split-second decisions just to stay competitive. We can't hold up a business deal or delay making that crucial first impression while we ask prospects to complete a 100-question Scantron form and bubble in their answers.

We don't have time for a committee to analyze the results. Life moves quickly. Business opportunities move even faster. We need to be swift in our actions to keep up.

What is the premium bonus for taking the time to read this book? The why question is answered! Character Coding reveals why you do what you do and shows you how to understand the people around you so you can thrive in business and life.

Why Six Character Codes?

My behavioral studies led me to create six Character Codes, because trying to fit everyone into the typical four-type model was too limiting. The four-type model had some people feeling left out. Additionally, trying to make people conform to a conventional identification based on a set of impersonal letters like those generated by the Myers-Briggs test was not only complicated but off-putting.

People prefer to create a visual mental image of themselves and others; that's how our brains work. So I named each of the Character Codes based on personality types familiar to most of us from our high school days. Visualize how each title conjures up an image of a particular type of individual:

>> The Class President
>> The Cheerleader

» The Actor

» The Scholar

» The Activist

» The Artist

Are you visualizing someone for each Character Code? Good! In the next section you'll see a Quickstart chart and sketches to get you going. In no time you'll be able to easily identify people and read them from across the room. Learn more about them in the following chapters, and you will be unstoppable in your client interactions.

An Introduction to the Character Codes

You are going to encounter every Character Code in life, and so it really helps to learn the other Codes in order to better understand and relate to them. You will take things far less personally, be a better communicator, and have a greater compassion for others.

And make no mistake, it is perfectly normal to recognize that there are just some people you get along with better than others. Yes, I said it. There are some people you are going to want to avoid.

So how does this knowledge pan out in work and play? In business it means knowing whom you want to attract as clients and how to serve them. In the corporate or sales environment it means being able to communicate effectively and advance quickly in your company.

In your personal life, it can mean the difference between selecting friends or a mate who really "gets" you. When I've taught my Character Codes in Relationships course, I've had clients say this newfound understanding saved their marriage or made them a better parent.

Want a quick sneak peek into which Character Code you might be? Check out these shortcut questions at http://charactercode .com/quiz. To help get you started, the chart that follows provides a short overview of each Character Code at a glance. Then, in the following chapters, I'll outline each of the Character Codes in detail, including how to use this information in your business and day-to-day life.

	Class President	Cheerleader	Actor
Driving Need	Certainty	Variety	Significance
Fast vs. Slow Processing	Faster	Faster	Faster
People vs. Task Oriented	Task	People	Both
Appearance	Conservative, classic, tasteful, class ring, black or solid colors, pant suits, tailored	Stylish, flirty, fun, full makeup, colors or pastels, "boy or girl next door"	Big hair, full makeup, showy, jewelry, dramatic, flashy, loud prints, sexy clothing
Presentation	Stands tall, alert, projects power, confidence, credibility, moves quickly, decisive	Friendly, upbeat, moves fast, toucher, hugger, works the room	High energy, animated, power, loud, drama, commanding presence
Speaking	Frank, direct, uses "I think" vs. "I feel," demanding, says "What's the bottom line?"	Talkers, blurters, TMI, emotional, motivational, optimistic	Loud talker, blurter, prone to exaggerate, animated story teller, sarcastic
Psyche	Wants to do things right, be in control, very specific, gets things done, ambitious	Persuasive, easily bored, feels distracted, overwhelmed, wants to be liked	Burning desire to do big things, craves attention or celebrity status, wants to be known
Issue to Overcome	Feeling trust	Feeling alive	Feeling seen
Childhood	Specific or right way to do things, never good enough	Good when performing or making people happy	Survived truly tough situations, had to fend for self
Inner Meanie (Critical Voice)	Severely critical, not good enough, demanding, perfectionist	Not important, conditional love, seeks validation & recognition	Inherently flawed, not good enough in all categories

	Scholar	Activist	Artist
Driving Need	Certainty	Connection	Significance
Fast vs. Slow Processing	Slower	Slower	Slower
People vs. Task Oriented	Task	People	Both
Appearance	Function over fashion, simple solid colors, little to no jewelry	Natural look, simple or no makeup, earthy colors and fibers, wears layers	Stylish, retro, eclectic, unique look, prefers fashion over function
Presentation	Knowledge, little eye contact, stands apart, thinking, rigid body stance	Calming energy, holds eye contact, hugger, stands close, fluid body stance	Too cool for words, reserved, distant, appears aloof or shy, observing
Speaking	Dislikes small talk, focuses on data, objective language, monotone	Feeling language, great listener, quiet calm voice, sensitive	Descriptive terms, strong opinions, quiet with bursts of passion
Psyche	Thinking, not feeling, routine, disconnect, binary language, wants evidence	Seeks calm, peaceful life, not a risk taker, not competitive, heartfelt	Unique point of view, deep feeling, sensing, solitary, retreats to imagination
Issue to Overcome	Feeling trust	Feeling loved	Feeling seen
Childhood	Rigid sense of right and wrong, surrounded by strict rules	Didn't feel understood, safe, or nurtured as a child, no security	Felt different, outsider, overlooked, undervalued
Inner Meanie (Critical Voice)	Not smart enough, haven't achieved enough or done it right	Not capable or brave enough, not special, smart, or talented	Fear of not really being special, of being just like everyone else

11

Character Coding with the Driving Needs

A key to master Character Coding includes distinguishing the driving needs that dictate much of our personal and professional behavior.

The Purpose of Driving Needs

Many philosophers and psychologists have studied the theory of basic human needs and desires. Depending on whom you've read, they may list 4, 7, or 11 or more human needs. The most widely known model of needs was created by twentieth-century psychologist Abraham Maslow, who preferred a hierarchy model that included basic human needs for survival. There are desires that extend beyond the obvious survival needs of nutrition and shelter. Animals share these basic needs. One of the things that sets us apart as humans is our driving needs, which can be as much of a commanding force in our behavior as an animal's instinct for survival.

If we are to understand ourselves and others, we must first understand how these needs impact our lives. The four driving needs that influence the majority of our decisions include *certainty*, *variety*, *significance*, and *connection*. In theory, our lives would be fulfilling if all these needs were being consistently satisfied.

What I have found, though, is that each Character Code has one driving need that exerts the most powerful influence in the lives of people in that Code. This driving need has such a strong pull that it impacts almost all decision making—the way people dress, their body posture or language, the way they speak, their interpersonal and business relationships—you name it. That primary need is running the individual's personal show. People are always trying to have their driving need satisfied. It is the filter through which they view all of life, and it exerts a powerful influence on all their actions.

When you identify and understand this driving need for yourself and the people around you, it is empowering. With awareness you will have the option to serve the need, moderate it, or even dismiss it if the situation warrants it. It will no longer blindly lead you through life, work, and play. Of course, it doesn't go away either, and so don't underestimate the influence of these driving needs.

When your client's driving need is met—for example, through your selling or marketing—you can expect a positive outcome. Every conflict I've seen has been caused by failing to understand or meet an individual's driving need. It is the basis not only for the creation of empowering relationships, but for all miscommunication and discord. Let's take a closer look at the four driving needs.

And remember, wherever you go, there you are.

—Confucius

The Four Driving Needs

A need is not a want. Wanting something in life is optional. A driving need is so primary that the individual will go to great lengths to make sure it is met. Life is not static, and these needs cannot be permanently satisfied through one action; and so we find ourselves constantly striving to serve that need. Think about your own needs and the needs of your clients as you read the following.

Certainty

Certainty is the need to know what is going to happen or a predictable pattern of events. Those who value certainty understand the consequences of an action. They prefer to know the requirements, the outcome, and the results—when it will end, the bottom line. If there is a domino effect in play, they need to anticipate how it will turn out. They don't appreciate surprises.

Of course, we all know there is no real certainty in life. That doesn't matter to the particular Character Code individuals who desire it. They will strive for tangible results in all their activities and often seek material wealth or belongings. They will do this because concrete items or a known plan of events provides real comfort, security, and peace of mind for these individuals.

Certainty is most desired by the Class President and Scholar Character Codes.

A Class President's Driving Need for Certainty. *Ellen has been an entrepreneur for decades and loves being her own boss, in charge of each day and creating her own future. She has worked hard to build a stable financial portfolio, has invested in real estate, and is a leader in her industry. Her greatest challenge in business has been finding staff that can keep up, and she has yet to find anyone that can run the office the way she does. She loves the freedom of being able to leave the office whenever she wants; however, she rarely does, as her "to-do" list is a mile long and she relishes getting things done. Ellen has an impeccable reputation with her clients for her high integrity and quality service.*

A Scholar's Driving Need for Certainty. *Steve is in middle management, is employed by a large corporation, and handles the technical project requirements for building data storage centers. He created a foolproof system for calculating the supplies, projected costs, and utility needs for each center, charting and graphing his calculations and reporting them back to his immediate supervisor. Steve takes the same route to work each morning, parks in the same spot, and eats lunch at precisely the same time each day. He has specific ideas regarding the right way to execute his job duties and the proper way to communicate with senior staff, and he expects his own staff to follow the system he has created.*

Variety

Variety is the need for fun and change. The individuals whose driving need is variety seek the excitement and anticipation—and even the uncertainty—from new thoughts, perceptions, and experiences. They desire adventure, surprises, and celebration, but this does not mean they are hedonists or simpleminded fun lovers. They are often creative, exuberant, and influential and are always looking for the next exciting event.

Now, life isn't always a party. However, for those that value variety as their driving need, the craving for excitement can be like a drug. The tedium and boring routine of a daily grind will feel like a death sentence to this type of individual.

Variety is most desired by the Cheerleader Character Code.

A Cheerleader's Driving Need for Variety. *Christina is always smiling and describes herself as a "serial entrepreneur." She was an independent rep in a direct sales business, launched a custom greeting card line, and dabbled in reviewing wines, and she is a licensed aesthetician. She volunteers at her children's school and helps raise much needed funds. Christina also serves on the board of several local charities, volunteers at the hospital, and cochairs a business networking group for women. Christina hasn't had her businesses grow to the level she'd like; however, she loves her full life and enjoys vacationing with her family in new destinations each year. She's always up for a new adventure.*

Significance

Significance speaks to one's driving need to feel special. Individuals with this need are compelled by the desire to be noticed for their talents and the traits that make them unique. Those who seek significance want to be regarded as an individual and not as part of the group. They are often struggling to be known for who they are and how they are seen.

Now, some prefer significance with a spotlight so that everyone sees them shine, such as the Actor; others are not looking for attention, such as the Artist. What they want is simply to not get lost in the crowd.

Significance is the most desired by the Actor and Artist Character Codes.

An Actor's Driving Need for Significance. *Tripp has worked in sales on straight commission for the last five years. He is young and determined and often comes across as cocky. He regularly exceeds his sales quotas, blowing the competition out of the water, and has been known to land large accounts after "wining and dining" the buyers. On occasion Tripp has caused conflict among his company's sales team, but he doesn't care as long as his name is at the top of the leader board. He loves being evaluated on his individual effort and avoids partnering with other sales team members, preferring to be a lone wolf. Tripp thinks his sales methods should* *be adopted companywide and has toyed with the idea of starting his own company.*

An Artist's Driving Need for Significance. *Fiona loves her work as a writer. She created a blog reviewing environmentally friendly products, designed her own graphics, and has built an online following with her "Fiona Finds . . ." newsletter. She is rarely recognized in public but has won online awards for her work. Fiona loves that she can work out of her home, listens to her favorite music as she works, and has decorated her office with her artwork and eclectic collection of throw pillows. She's been looking into what it would take to start a nonprofit to educate about sustainability and ecofriendly products. Her hobby is making stained glass.*

Connection

Connection is the need to feel another person's humanity. Individuals in this category have the need to develop close, personal relationships and feel nurtured. They need to really know another person. They desire to be similarly understood in return. Those who seek connection as their driving need place the highest value on the personal touch in relationships and possess great emotional depth. In such a relationship, be it personal or business, they will feel most empowered.

These people are typically sensitive souls who take their time getting to know someone. Similarly, they make their decisions slowly and carefully.

Connection is most desired by the Activist Character Code.

An Activist's Driving Need for Connection. *Scotty has always loved being around people, talking to them, and learning more about their lives. He worked as a car salesman for a while, and although he rarely sold a car, the customers loved him, and his colleagues described him as having the "best attitude." Scotty decided to leave the car dealership so that he could go back to school to work as a counselor helping families cope after divorce. It took a long time to earn his certificate, as he attended school in the evening* *and led museum tours during the day. Initially, he struggled to build a private practice but then thrived when he landed a job serving families through the local courthouse. His clients describe him as the "best listener."*

Take a few minutes to reflect on what you've just learned about the driving needs. What do you think is your driving need? How about those of your spouse, best friend, closest colleague, and best client?

An important piece to Character Coding is appreciating the impact that a driving need has on people's behavior, including how people "show up" in daily life.

Identifying the Character Codes

Everyone makes some kind of judgment when meeting a person for the first time. That's where the saying "You never get a second chance to make a first impression" comes from. What is rarely explained is why this occurs, and we'll cover that in great detail in Chapter 2 so that you can attract your ideal clients. For now, I want you to understand that being able to quickly read a client from across the room is largely based on the first impression.

So in the six chapters dedicated to each Character Code, I'll cover the three components of a first impression: *appearance, presentation,* and *speaking.* I often refer to these three components as your personal branding. Whether you are an entrepreneur or executive, you personally represent the company you stand behind, and the merits of that business are often measured by your appearance and behavior.

Once we have identified and understand those three components and specific traits, we can take the next step to knowing the individual's *psyche*—whether our own or that of others—and learn the why aspect of the behavior in which we are so interested.

The combination of appearance, presentation, and speaking style lets us know which Character Code someone is, and the psyche component lets us know who they are, what they're about, and how to best attract them and serve them as clients. It is the meaning behind our message.

Putting the Character Codes to Practical Use

As you read the different traits for each Character Code in the dedicated chapters, remember that the Code isn't a checklist where you have to satisfy every item listed. This isn't a profiling system that wants to stick you in a box or postulate that there are only six types of people in the world. Character Coding is designed so that you will recognize yourself in one or more of the Codes and then use your newfound understanding to better communicate and, ultimately, improve your success in business and in life. The Character Code System is a powerful tool for everyday human understanding; remember the driving needs and see what resonates for you.

When you know which Character Codes define you and come to understand your psyche, you can choose to be much more forgiving and patient with yourself. Once you know how you behave when stressed or out of balance, you can make changes to soften the effect. And you will gain empathy and understanding for other Character Codes and become more tolerant and understanding of them as well.

When it comes to communicating with your audience, attracting your ideal client, and marketing your business, Character Coding assists you in knowing the dreams, fears, joys, and concerns of the people with whom you want to connect. When you know your ideal client on that level, all your communication will be much more effective. This knowledge applies to all your business relationships: you'll be better equipped to understand your partner, boss, or coworker, too.

There is no "right" Character Code, and one is not better than the other. We all have our strengths and challenges, and we all show up in varying states of balance or imbalance. Awareness is the first step toward true self-acceptance and understanding. When you have achieved that, you will experience the kind of self-esteem that is rock solid and makes you unstoppable in the world.

Finally, note that my Character Code System is shared with you in the spirit of compassion, without judgment, shame, or blame.

It isn't about being "better than" or without flaws. This system is about discerning and developing an appreciation of who you are, playing to your strengths, and applying your new knowledge in your dealings with other human beings. Please use it with the same compassion with which it was created for you and then rock all your client connections!

How to Read a Client Now

Now that you have been introduced to the driving needs and are beginning to learn the Character Codes, remember to:

» Mentally visualize what personality traits come to mind just from the titles Class President, Cheerleader, Actor, Scholar, Activist, and Artist.

» Notice which driving need most impacts your behavior: certainty, variety, significance, or connection.

» Begin to observe how these driving needs are impacting those around you, particularly potential clients.

» Consider that a driving need doesn't have to be realistic or even rational to greatly influence your actions.

» Observe what feelings come up as you begin to realize that how you show up in your appearance, presentation, and speaking style reflects who you are and what you care about?

Chapter 2 will break down the importance of the first impression, discuss the assumptions your clients make about you, identify deal breakers to avoid, and explain how to showcase your personal branding for client attraction. Immediately following that chapter are the six chapters detailing each of the Character Codes.

Take the following action steps now:

» Take the online shortcut quiz "Which Character Code Are You?" at http://charactercode.com/quiz. It will shed light on why you do what you do and will take less than five minutes.

» Download the resource "Driving Needs for Each Character Code and How to Keep Your Clients Happy" at http://charactercode.com/happyclients.

» Access the "Character Codes at a Glance" chart in color at http://charactercode.com/ataglance.

TWO

The Challenges We Face in Attracting Clients

If You Build It, Will They Come?

LOVE A GOOD CHALLENGE. I like the feeling that comes from seeing a problem, figuring out a strategy to solve it, and then realizing the results. I'll bet you do, too.

Every business owner, executive, or entrepreneur has the same challenge: generate revenue, which typically means having clients who will buy their goods or services. In the movie *Field of Dreams*, a voice whispers to farmer Ray Kinsella, "If you build it, he will come." Ray builds a baseball diamond in his cornfield and then waits as old-time players show up. Meanwhile, he is near to losing his farm. Ray is fortunate; the baseball diamond and the phantom ball players become a draw for paying customers at $20 a head. His farm is saved from foreclosure. The whispered remark from this movie became a mantra for many in business: "Build it and they will come."

The bottom-line message is clear; there is no success in business without a client base. Many have jumped into starting a business from a simple idea, took the blind leap, and then watched their business fail. It turned out that there wasn't a client base or that the product didn't solve a need the customer was aware of. I've experienced both outcomes—the failure and the success. What was the difference? For the success, I used Character Coding to make sure I created a product that served my clients' driving need, and clients lined up at the door.

I love the build-it-and-they-will-come model, as long as it isn't a blind leap. Use the Character Codes to make wise decisions. It is classic problem-and-solution thinking, and it works. So let us assume you have accomplished the first basic business building steps. Now the question is, how do we attract clients and close the deal in order to realize our dreams?

Well, it really starts with you personally. Whether you generate a client base in person (meeting one-on-one, networking, speaking to groups, attending trade shows, participating in live events), do it online (Internet marketing, e-mail, ads, social media), or use any other marketing means, there is a face, a persona, an energy or attitude that you communicate to your potential client base.

This is why you need to be clear about who you are, what you are about, and what your message is (above and beyond just your product or business model). Your potential customers need to know that you can solve their problem; they want to like you, your company, or your brand, and they need to know the quickest way to say yes to your product or service.

> *A good basic selling idea, involvement and relevancy, of course, are as important as ever, but in the advertising din of today, unless you make yourself noticed and believed, you ain't got nothin'.*
>
> **—Leo Burnett, legendary advertising executive**

Here is an example. Three former corporate desk jockeys are downsized and find they're unable to land another job. Each signs up for business and marketing training to become a social media coach. They are all about the same age with similar experience and find themselves now competing for clients along with every other business owner in the marketplace searching for the entrepreneurial promised land.

Tom with the Geek Hotline. *Tom uses Character Coding to realize that as a Scholar, he doesn't want to have to attend every networking event and is happiest working from home with his laptop. When he does meet people in person or online, he realizes that some think he is a little geeky, and so he decides to use that as a strength in his branding. He chooses Cheerleader women entrepreneurs as* *his ideal clients and designs marketing that identifies their pain of being overwhelmed, having too much to juggle, and being burdened by social media as just another "to do" on the list and a tech nightmare to boot! He creates a "Geek Hotline" and uses headlines such as "Geek It Done for You: Social Media Solutions for Business Superwomen." He quickly spots his ideal clients whenever he does choose to network, greeting them in a fun and upbeat way with "Hi, I'm Tom, your Geek-for-Hire for Women-on-the-Go. How can I shorten your to-do list today so you can have more fun?" Tom builds a small business doing what he loves.*

Adam with Excellent Customer Service. *Adam studied hard when he took his training, and he diligently applies everything he learned. He jumps into networking and online marketing, creates products, buys ads, and rents office space for his new business. He uses the templates, copy, and standard business formulas he learned. The costs rack up, but the clients are nowhere to be seen. Adam is trying everything but keeps running into the same problem: he is indistinguishable from everyone else. He is embarrassed when he attends social networking events and finds he's standing next to five other entrepreneurs, all specializing in social media. Adam admits he would be hard-pressed to say why you should work with him versus any of the other experts. They're all saying the same thing, promising fair prices and excellent customer service. He doesn't stand out. The cost and the lack of clients become too discouraging, and Adam folds his entrepreneurial tent.*

Sandra with Successful Networking. *Sandra quickly realizes the field is crowded. Everyone is now a social media expert, and she wonders what will set her apart. As a combination Class President–Cheerleader Character Code, she is great with strategy, excellent at getting things done, and a darn good networker. She knows how to make a great first impression, loves meeting new people, and is less interested in handling all the minute details. Sandra decides to play to her strengths, creates a social media matrix designed to market to women consumers, and builds an overseas outsourcing* *team to handle the execution. She networks, makes connections, and sets up meetings with small businesses and corporations that are looking to contract their social media. Sandra consistently presents well—she uses her research on the phenomenal buying power of women consumers and the exploding growth in social media commerce and makes sure people understand how much time consumers spend online and how her matrix and outsourcing team provide the missing ingredients for a big piece of this pie. Sandra's business is thriving.*

Tom and Sandra understood the principles you'll learn throughout this book:

>> Use Character Coding to know who you are and how to play to your strengths and set yourself up to win.

>> Identify an ideal Character Code client and make sure your product, business model, or message answers a problem the client needs solved.

>> Serve your client's driving need and provide an easy way for the client to say yes.

>> Understand the importance of your *first impressions* whether online or in person.

You are going to want to master the art of making a successful first impression if you want to do what Sandra and Tom did: show up before the world and visibly express how you are the expert at what you do—your greatness, if you will—and why your potential customers or clients ought to be beating a path to your door. Yes, if you do the work to build yourself and your business, they *will* come.

First Impressions, Professional and Personal

I knew a professional who said, "I know I come off like a jerk when people first meet me, but later on they see I'm really a nice guy inside." Being a nice person—that's the only personal quality that really matters, right? Actually, that isn't the case. The truth is, most people won't take—or simply don't have—the time to get past that first impression to get to know you better and then decide later on whether or not they like you. What most people do is make a few split-second assumptions, then decide whether or not they want to get to know you, either personally or professionally. At that point their mind is made up and they are done.

Whether or not you think this is fair, I invite you to consider why people operate this way. It is all about biology and survival. Our nervous system has been programmed to quickly assess situations to see if they are safe or not. This includes making assumptions about people. Is it safe for me to ride alone in the elevator with that person? Can I trust this new bookkeeper? Should I give out my cell phone number or e-mail address?

We make these all-important snap decisions based on first impressions of people, situations, products, services, and online communications every day. This is why the Character Code System was designed to be a visual system and serve the needs of our fast-paced society and ever-shortening attention span.

These snap decisions are commonly based on a visual image or perception that we assimilate into the database of our brain: that first impression becomes either intuitive acceptance or distrust. Discovering the implications of the first impression is paramount in our businesses, as well as in our personal lives. You don't need a social scientist to prove first impressions are scientifically sound. You just *know* it.

> *. . . perception becomes reality. This implies that you ought to manage your image and reputation as well as your actual work.*
>
> **—Jeffrey Pfeffer, PhD**
> **Stanford Graduate School of Business**

Showing Up

First impressions are often lasting impressions. People usually stop processing new information or perceptions about you once they have reached their first impression, even if you start showing up in a new way. As you read in the following chapters on the individual Character Codes, you will discover that some types are more open to noticing a change in your behavior, while others go to great lengths to prove their initial assumptions about you were correct.[1]

That is huge.

Are you beginning to realize that first impressions are about more than just looking pleasant, having a warm smile, or using a firm handshake? There is a deeply rooted psychological and biological basis for the persistence of the first impression. Therefore, it is most important that you make the greatest first impression possible. Since you usually only have one shot at showing up, you want people to make the most positive judgment about you.

You Control First Impressions

On what information are first impressions for likability formed? You may find it surprising to learn they are largely made by assessing visual input.[2] And why do we care about likability? Because it influences the yes or no response from a potential client.

Bob Burg, bestselling coauthor of *The Go Giver* and author of *Endless Referrals*, says: "All things being equal, people will do business with, and refer business to, those people they know, like and trust."

The "know, like and trust" factor begins with the first impression, and it is important to know that the breakdown listed below is filtered differently by each Character Code. In other words, each Character Code applies his or her own meaning to the message you are sending. For example, a well-dressed Class President in a suit would be perceived as professional and classy by another Class President—and likely be perceived as professional but stuffy by an Activist. A Cheerleader in a floral dress might be perceived as fun and stylish by an Artist but not taken seriously by a Scholar.

Here is more on the breakdown of first impressions for likability[3]:

What We See

» *Fifty-five percent of your first impression is based on your appearance and presentation. Appearance includes your* hair, makeup, jewelry, nails, clothing, accessories, and shoes. *Presentation* includes your body language, posture, facial expressions, and physical communication.

What Sounds We Hear

» Thirty-eight percent is your *vocal tone*, the sound of your voice, volume, quality, pitch, and resonance.

What Words We Hear

» Seven percent is your *speaking style*—the actual words and phrases you express.

Appearance

Your appearance is by far the most important aspect of your first impression. It isn't about being conventionally pretty, nor is it about your age or your size. It represents the *choices* you make in how you show up. It is like the packaging for a product or an advertisement for a service. How you choose to package your external appearance should showcase your inner value. We all have inherent value, but are you expressing yours externally? It would be great if everyone could see the gem you are inside, but first impressions are based on what the eye sees, and that is the packaging. Make sure you visually express your value.

> *It is only shallow people who do not judge by appearances.*
> **—Oscar Wilde, Irish poet, novelist, and critic**

A mistake I often see people make is in thinking that the *only* way to express value or make a good first impression is to wear a classy or expensive suit or dress. While it is true that kind of apparel can send a professional message, if it isn't you, then seek an alternative. There are so many options today to put your best foot forward and still show up feeling empowered. I suggest you stick to being you. I'm not advocating that you wear your comfy pajamas to work, just that we can all be a sparkling and shiny version of ourselves while still being true to who we are inside. In the dedicated Character Code chapters, I will share suggested items so you can work with your natural look while helping your ideal client feel comfortable and trusting when meeting you for the first time. These are smart, savvy, and subtle suggestions to use as you consider your audience or the ideal clients you want to attract. Below is an example of how to put this into action.

Your Appearance in the First Impression

In one of my businesses I was marketing to a Cheerleader-Activist Character Code combo. As a Class President I was happy wearing black clothing all the time; however, the color black wasn't appealing to my Cheerleader clients (it made me appear too austere), and it was a turnoff to my Activist clients (who almost never wear black). Now, I wasn't about to start wearing floral skirts or a yoga wrap, because it wouldn't feel like me at all. So I choose to start using dark blue as my "new black" and added dark brown and some gray to mix up my wardrobe and lighten my appearance. It was a subtle shift that made me more approachable for my ideal clients, and yet I still felt empowered as a Class President. The result: my private consulting practice was filled with my ideal Character Code clients that came up to me and said, "I have to work with you." Of course, there's more to attracting clients than just how you look—but I don't want you to overlook or underestimate the communication of your appearance—first the impact it has on you, and second the impact it has on others.

Those things we care most about are reflected in our appearance, and so we are constantly giving clues to others about how we want to be treated. Here is a breakdown to give you a clearer idea of how to identify those clues—in yourself and others. Each of these items will be covered in detail for each Character Code in the following chapters.

>> **Hair.** Hair is a great indicator of a person's Character Code. Hair length, style, type of hair care product, coloring, neat or disheveled grooming, and regularity of cuts are all

assessment features for Character Coding. For men, this also includes whether they are well groomed and whether they are clean shaven.

» **Makeup.** Makeup speaks loudly and clearly about a person's Character Code. Some may wear makeup because they enjoy it and others because they think it is expected or required for work. Most people form an impression about a woman by noting if she is wearing a lot, a little, or no makeup at all.

» **Jewelry.** Choice of jewelry is extremely personal, from costume jewelry to a one-of-a-kind designer piece. When you see someone wearing jewelry (or not), it provides insight into who they are and what they care about. It is not only the style but the amount of jewelry they wear. Complimenting people on their jewelry is one of the easiest ways to start a conversation in a networking setting. It is nonthreatening and a great icebreaker.

» **Clothing.** Choice in clothing broadcasts who we are: the style, color, fashion sense, and care we put into dressing ourselves. It doesn't have to be costly to look pulled together. Our driving need contributes to why we select the clothing items we choose to own and what they mean to us.

» **Accessories.** Your choice of purse, bag, or briefcase is more than just about a way to carry your belongings. Right down to the cover for your iPad, your accessories are part of your personal branding, a reflection of your individual style. Small, large, fashionable, worn, pricey or knock-off, all provide additional insight into your particular Character Code.

» **Nails.** Attention to fingernails sheds light when it comes to Character Coding and is often a great clue when typing people all wearing the same uniform. Length, paint color, and patterns differentiate individual Character Codes. Meticulous? Chewed and bitten? A man with buffed nails? Often the little details can be so telling.

» **Shoes.** Sneakers, high heels, flats, oxfords, platforms, wing tips. Clean, scuffed, shined, ignored or lovingly cared for;

footwear provides many insights into personality. Each of the Character Codes wears and cares for footwear quite differently.

I still have my feet on the ground. I just wear better shoes.

—Oprah Winfrey

Presentation

Your presentation plays a significant role in your first impression and is largely assessed by visual means. The way you carry yourself, your facial expressions, your hand gestures, and the way you move your body combine to form a language all its own. These actions communicate a distinct message to the viewer in a first impression—as do texting, looking impatient, slouching, making nervous repetitive gestures, and maintaining eye contact.

How things look on the outside of us depends on how things are on the inside of us.

—Anonymous

If you are attending a networking event for business professionals and want to meet new contacts, that means you need to be approachable. A very common presentation mistake is crossing your arms over your chest, which looks to others like a defensive shield or even like you are antisocial. If you are holding up a wall or texting, the message you're sending is that you're busy. No one will want to interrupt to talk to you. Neither one is very appropriate for networking! Below is an example of this in action.

Your Presentation in the First Impression

When I first started speaking, I always looked so serious. It wasn't that I didn't have a good time; I just really wanted to share my information with the members of my audience and make sure they "got it." A typical default facial expression for a Class President is to be thinking, and that can come across as looking stern. I had to learn to bring out more of my Cheerleader side and smile. After I was done presenting, I would immediately begin packing up my laptop and PowerPoint clicker. After all, as a Class President, I value efficiency. I quickly noticed that this action made me unapproachable to the audience members that were lining up and wanting to connect with me after the presentation. I learned to immediately move into the "meet-and-greet" mode following a speech. The packing could wait.

Presentation contributes to that 55 percent of a first impression based on what we see. This influences prospective clients who are deciding whether or not they like you, want to connect with you, or want to work with you. In the following chapters I'll cover your posture, hand gestures, eye contact, facial expressions, movement, pacing, and the energy, or *vibe*, you project. Each of these physical traits is very telling about you as a person and part of Character Coding.

Speaking

The words you choose and how you deliver them is also a key part of your first impression. What is interesting is that the way you deliver your message is five times more impactful than the actual words you use when it comes to likability.[4] Most people spend a lot of time working on the wording but don't realize the negative impact of a monotone voice, a high-pitched squeak, a nasal tone, or a harsh vocal quality. Vocal coaches will encourage you to breathe, open your mouth, and move your jaw. Those things can have a big impact, particularly over the phone, as many people tense up when required to make calls—especially in the sales industry.

To speak and to speak well are two things. A fool may talk, but a wise man speaks.

—Ben Jonson, dramatist, poet, actor

Listening to the words that people use and their vocal delivery provides great insight into their Character Code. If you pay attention, you will see how they are shouting out their driving need through the way they communicate. They're just waiting for you to notice.

Your Speaking in the First Impression

If I need to get something done and am focused and not paying attention to the people around me, I will default to my Class President mode of speaking very directly, in short sentences, with abrupt endings expressing my desire to "bottom-line" it. Sometimes this is effective, and other times it is not—it depends on your audience and the situation. If I'm in my Cheerleader mode, my voice actually gets higher pitched, it has more lift at the ends of sentences, and my language will be more friendly and playful. In the first situation I'm clearly expressing that I want you to dazzle me with certainty and get the issue resolved quickly and decisively. In the second situation I'm showcasing that I'm ready for fun and adventure.

It doesn't mean that words don't matter—they do. However, if "content were king," there would have been a line out of my biochemistry teacher's classroom trying to get in, instead of the mad rush to escape whenever the lecture was completed. If you want to share a message and see that it lands effectively, whether you are a speaker, entrepreneur, or sales professional, make sure you consider what you say, how it is presented, and how you "package" it.

The trouble with talking too fast is you may say something you haven't thought of yet.

—Ann Landers

Speaking is a great way to confirm people's Character Codes in addition to what you have already noticed based on their appearance and presentation. Are they articulate? Do they have a good vocabulary? Do they express their thoughts confidently, mumble, stutter, or use slang? What people say and how they say it provides telling insight into who they are and how they think.

Psyche

Psyche was the Greek goddess of the soul. Psychology defines the psyche as the sum total of our conscious and unconscious mind: how we came to be who we are, what we value, and how we understand and use our strengths. In Character Coding, interpreting the psyche reveals the why behind the way we show up for the world. The psyche is the source of our choices in our appearance, presentation, and speaking style that, together, contribute to our individual Character Code.

The psyche component of the Character Code System explains why we care about the first impression and why it's important to understand the motivations fueling our decisions. There is a "Psyche" section in each Character Code chapter to help reveal the driving need, the impact of nature versus nurture, character traits, and our behavior under stress and in conflict.

Each Character Code has its own critical voice, which I describe as the *inner meanie*. Learning that you're not the only person who suffers from negative self-talk, and that the inner meanie talks similarly to others who share your Character Code, can be liberating. The inner meanie never speaks the truth and operates from the mental space where fear, doubt, and insecurity reside. Understanding the inner meanie—not just your own but that of your ideal Character Code client—will hugely impact your marketing and customer service.

Also included in the "Psyche" section are character traits, conflict, stress and emotions, health and wellness, jobs and career, marketing and sales, and ideal clients for each individual Character Code. At the end of each chapter, the best and worst ways to make a first impression for that particular Character Code are outlined. Knowing this will determine if you will attract people to you or push them away.

The Judgment Call

A judgment call occurs within several seconds of a first impression.[5] This call occurs whenever a person sees you for the first time. That means when you are sitting in an office, getting out of your car, shopping at the grocery store, making a conference presentation—any time another person takes particular notice of you. If you are meeting someone in a work setting, the judgment call isn't necessarily when you step into the person's office. Instead, it might be when the person sees you waiting in the lobby or walking down the hall toward his or her office. A job interview can be over before you sit down.

First impressions and subsequent judgment calls are made almost instantly when visiting your website, when a client reads your business proposal, or when a consumer views a product in its packaging. If your website doesn't lead viewers to the information they seek immediately, they are gone.[6] If your business proposal has typographical errors or is printed with a blurry inkjet printer, your prospect may reject you as unprofessional. If your product is packaged in a plastic clamshell and your customer prefers recyclable packaging, it may cost you the sale. This is why marketing departments spend so much time and money trying to figure out what will best appeal to potential clients. With Character Coding you have the advantage. Once you read the chapter for your ideal Character Code client, you can make informed business decisions. Mere seconds may make all the difference between a yes and no response from prospective clients.[7, 8]

How does that first impression of your appearance, presentation, and speaking style translate into a decision? By the judgment value that your potential client places on any or all of the assumptions listed below:

>> Trustworthiness

>> Confidence, credibility

>> Financial status

>> Education level, intelligence

>> Sophistication, success

>> Family history

>> Relationship status, sexual identification

>> Religious background, morality

If you are thinking, "Wow, that's quite a few decision points," you're right. But consider that not all come into play every time, and they are never equally weighted. The individual Character Codes develop their own list of priorities, based on their individual driving need—in other words, what they value most in life. For example, an Actor Character Code may be more concerned with your financial status and confidence, a Scholar with your intelligence and education level, an Activist with your trustworthiness and family status.

Making these assumptions in a quick first impression doesn't mean that a judgment call is always right; it's just that *it is always made.* Understanding this two-step decision-making process—how first impressions are formed and how they inevitably lead to a judgment call—is key to successful communication in business and your personal life.

Go to http://charactercode.com/assumptions if you want to see the assumptions in action through pictures.

Deal Breakers

It won't matter how well you know your potential clients or how quickly you can spot which Character Code they are if you are engaging in any of the deal breakers listed in the next section. Why? Because if you sabotage the first impression in person, in print, in products, or online, your potential client is long gone before you even realize it.

As entrepreneurs and executives, we are personal brand ambassadors for our business or company. We are the face of our organization, and the way we show up often decides the deal before a product or terms have even been discussed.

Now, before you start thinking you need a complete personal makeover or years of finishing school, let me share my philosophy. I'm not encouraging you to be a puppet or suggesting you dress up in costume. I believe the most successful individuals are simply themselves—just the best version of who they are. They are aware of how they come across and how they need to connect with others. They also know that not everyone may be their ideal client or customer.

In the next several chapters devoted to each Character Code, I discuss each one's strengths and challenges in great detail. I don't suggest that a Scholar Character Code suddenly start behaving like a Cheerleader Character Code. However, we can always show up as our best selves, and I want you to be successful. I don't want your brilliance overlooked or your first impression spoiled because of some faux pas you made and weren't even aware of.

Avoid Sabotaging Your Success Before You Have Even Said a Word

Below are some general first-impression deal breakers you can avoid when it comes to your appearance and personal branding:

>> **Poor hygiene.** Most people have this covered, and yet when it occurs, it is a real stinker of a deal breaker. You want to always put your best foot forward and not offend. Think breath, body odor, and bad hair days. Some of the Character Codes are less concerned with these issues, but everyone needs to pay attention to them.

>> **Style.** We all have our own style, and as you study the Character Codes, you'll know what each person's style means and the message the person is trying to send you. Regardless of your personal style, whether you wear a suit and tie or a floral dress, looking "pulled together" goes a long way. Little details matter, like scuffed shoes, worn belts, or clothing that is too big or too tight.

Fashions fade, style is eternal.

—Yves Saint Laurent, French fashion designer

>> **Awareness.** How are you coming across? Do you stand too close or too far away? Are you always serious or always smiling? Do you really see the person standing in front of you? How is your message being received, and is the person listening to you? The answers to these questions should vary based on the individual you are talking to—that's what makes it a conversation. Being unaware of how you are being received is the deal breaker.

>> **Speaking style.** From rarely speaking up to stealing the show to always interrupting to "hotdogging" the conversation; long pauses, no active listening skills, poor enunciation, a monotone voice, or harsh language—any and all are first-impression deal breakers.

First-impression faux pas also extend to your product packaging and online marketing. Consider these two examples.

» **Electronic first impressions.** You only have seconds to grab the attention of potential customers and keep them on your website or get them to continue reading your e-mail marketing. Make sure your brand clearly represents who you are and connects with your ideal Character Code client. The colors you select, layout, images, typefaces, use of white space—all form a composite call to action.

» **Product packaging.** If your product isn't "wrapped" in a package that connects with your ideal Character Code client, it won't be purchased. Make sure the shape, color, title, language, and size of the package speak to the Character Code you are marketing to for optimal results. Selling to an Activist? Your packaging had better be ecofriendly. Selling designer clothing to Class Presidents? That hanger had better be distinctive. Use the "Psyche" section at the end of each Character Code chapter to understand how to reach your ideal client.

You want to know why your product, service, or information is top-notch in your industry. It takes work to create something that is well developed and will create explosive sales. Reward all that hard work by investing some time and energy in creating a fabulous first impression not only in person, but in your marketing, product packaging, and presentation.

Showing Up for Business and Life

So why do we care about first impressions? Because this is how we show up, how we communicate who we are and what we care about, to the rest of the world. Because we want to make a good impression so people will like and respect us, become our friends or our business partners or clients. Because we want people to make favorable judgment calls about us.

Whatever the type of first impression, whether it is made in person, by your products or services, or in your print or online presence, it's always about you. Your persona is part of everything you are and everything you do. Always make it the best you can be.

Remember from the Introduction when I described the period of my life when I didn't care how I was showing up? I was sending the message that I didn't care to all the people I met, and they reflected it right back at me. What was I thinking? It wasn't reasonable to expect anything else. When I started showing up for myself, the response from the outside world was amazing. It fed into a positive feedback loop of encouragement and success.

How we package ourselves matters, not because of the brand-name clothing or expensive accessories we wear, but because of the assumptions people make about who we are. Our personal branding tells the world how to treat us, and all those around us are doing the same thing, just screaming out who they are, telling us what they need.

When you understand this—not only about yourself, but about others—you are better positioned to communicate with your audience. Having your message land, hit home, and speak to people in their language is the secret behind effective marketing and outrageous sales (and successful personal relationships, for that matter).

Ultimately, it all boils down to communication. Knowing who you are and who your audience is will unlock the doors to success. The Character Codes will help you unlock those doors by showing you how to understand and communicate with others in ways you never imagined. Build it and they will come!

How to Read a Client Now

Now that you appreciate the impact of a great first impression to attract clients, remember to:

» Pay attention to all aspects of a first impression (appearance, presentation, speaking style) to make the most of your opportunity.

» Be mindful that what people see is more relevant than what they hear and that what they hear is five times more impactful than the actual words you speak when it comes to likability.

» Know that a judgment call will be made, influence what you can, and let go of the rest. Be the shiny version of you.

» Review the assumptions and deal breakers so that you always put your best foot forward. Being informed is powerful. Awareness is even better.

» Don't feel like you have to please everyone or be liked by everyone. Individual Character Codes view the world through their own filter, and you only need to attract one ideal Character Code client. Read the "Psyche" section in the next several chapters and make informed business decisions.

It is essential to read about each Character Code and not just your own in order to effectively select your ideal client. In Chapter 3 you will learn how to identify a Class President Character Code. This will include all the details you need to better communicate with, connect to, and read Class Presidents from across the room.

Take the following action steps now:

» Download the resource "Deal Maker—Where to Focus in the First Impression" at http://charactercode.com/firstimpression.

» Access the "Assumptions in Action" to visually see the assumptions via pictures. Make your own judgment call at http://charactercode.com/assumptions.

THREE

The Class President Character Code

Actions Speak Louder Than Words

NAMED THIS FIRST Character Code the Class President to help you get a vision in your head of someone who is successful and who appears thoughtfully pulled together—perhaps even buttoned-down—always a professional, constantly driven. A leader.

All these characteristics suggest that Class Presidents have an inner desire to show up, to always strive to do things to the best of their ability. They want to do things "right." This trait may have come from being taught as a child that there is a specific *right* way to perform a task. Speaking of which, Class Presidents are very task oriented. Their driving need is for certainty. They like being in control, knowing what is going to happen, and seeing it unfold along a predictable path.

You have already identified your own personal driving need. Are you a Class President? Do you know people who are Class Presidents? Now, using the three components of the first impression described in Chapter 1—appearance, presentation, and speaking style—here is how to read a Class President from across the room.

Appearance

As we discuss all six of the Character Codes, I'll break down their appearance into sections so that you have a clear idea of how to identify them in a crowd. I consider this their "personal branding," and it is a key component of the first impression. You can learn a lot about what people care about as reflected in their appearance, including how they want to be treated. You don't need to check off every item to confirm you are a particular Character Code. Each chapter outlines the typical trends and traits that will help you to identify your Character Code and that of others.

Hair

The Class President woman often wears her hair in a tasteful bob, which I call newscaster's hair. Regardless of its length or style, however, it is typically well styled, conservative, and tasteful. If her hair is long, it may be worn up or in a chic French twist for business. She may have a shorter cut, especially as she ages, that will always look polished and pulled together.

For male Class Presidents, the look is classic and short. Many choose a no-fuss cut that showcases their conservative style and keeps the attention on the business at hand.

Class President men are most often clean shaven. If they do wear facial hair, it will be neatly trimmed.

Makeup

The Class President woman will typically wear full makeup whenever she leaves the house, but it is not too heavy. She is stylish and fashionable. She will be more concerned with portraying a timeless, professional appearance than following the current hip trend. You will never see a Class President wear extreme colors on any part of her face—no big rosy cheeks for her. Her overall look is classic.

Jewelry

Here again, the Class President woman's taste in jewelry is best described as classic, timeless, and tasteful. She prefers silver or gold and loves two-tone pieces in either lustrous or matte finishes. Her jewelry emphasizes clean, clear lines and is symmetrical. She loves David Yurman designs. A single strand of pearls is a trademark piece.

If she wears diamonds or crystals, the pieces are tasteful and classy, never so large as to be overwhelming. She occasionally wears romantic jewelry, but only if it looks luxurious and has a rich, classic look. She is unlikely to wear natural jewelry, such as stones bound with leather.

Class President men don't wear decorative jewelry. The items they do wear will have a purpose or meaning behind them, such as a large class ring, a trophy ring, or a wedding band with clean, classic lines. If they wear a watch, it would be a powerful and expensive piece, such as a Rolex. They are the most likely of all the Character Codes to wear cuff links. Both the Class President woman and man are interested in conveying a sense of power and success rather than wearing what is regarded as trendy, pretty, or nonessential.

Clothing

Since it is the power color, Class Presidents are the most likely to wear black. Both men and women may elect to wear tailored suits. If not black, they prefer solid colors over patterns but will sometimes wear a pinstripe. Wearing a button-down oxford shirt or other tailored clothing is common for both men and women. In casual or outdoor settings, a Class President male can be easily spotted by his collared polo shirt.

Class President women avoid ruffles, as well as floral prints and anything overly flirty or revealing. She prefers classic lines and a crisp, conservative style in dresses, skirts, tops, and trousers. If there is a choice between dressing up or dressing down, she will always dress up. She's the woman sporting a French manicure and wearing the matching jogging suit at the gym.

She is a fan of blazers and trench coats in cooler weather and will shy away from baggy sweaters or parkas. Typically, she will not wear a long skirt, preferring slacks instead. If she does wear a skirt, it will be tailored and more likely to fall right above the knee (but no shorter). She is not fond of dresses unless they are tailored and classic.

The Class President man is one of the sharpest-looking guys in the room. He is comfortable in a suit. His clothing style is polished, typically in a monotone color palette and with a power tie. He may wear a dress shirt with a white collar and white cuffs or a pinstripe shirt. On the rare occasions that he wears jeans, they are a designer brand and have a dark wash. A more typical casual look for the Class President man would be khaki slacks with a polo shirt and a blazer.

Accessories

The Class President woman carries a more traditional than fashionable purse, bag, or briefcase. Her purse has clean lines and is conservative in color. She may be a fan of Chanel or Louis Vuitton handbags. Her briefcase would also be classic, stylish, and efficient, including space for her laptop or iPad.

The male Class President does not have a man bag but instead will carry a traditional briefcase with black leather. He will consider a briefcase required gear for work, and it will add to his overall professional image.

Nails

The Class President woman prefers a French manicure. Her nails are just slightly longer than her fingertips. Her pedicures are often French style as well. Unlike other Character Codes, she typically avoids having her nails painted in patterns or designs. Class President women will often consider getting a manicure or pedicure as another item to check off their to-do list and will want to make it as efficient as possible.

Class President men are unlikely to want to spend time in a spa, preferring to perform their own personal care. They wear their nails neatly trimmed and avoid having them buffed or painted.

Shoes

The Class President woman regularly wears a black pump, sometimes with a higher heel. This is the classic look for her. Other possibilities would be neutral colors or two-tones, but typically solids and without embellishments. Boots are a possibility as long as they are sleek and not bulky or cumbersome.

Class President men wear classic black or brown dress shoes that coordinate with their clothing.

Bear in mind, Class Presidents do not overdo anything when it comes to their appearance. Their appearance choices are dictated by their desire to project their professionalism.

Presentation

The Class President's presentation style reflects this Code's desire for certainty and stability. Class President men and women love to project their power, always communicating the message that they are in control of the situation. They typically stand erect and have good posture, demonstrating their alertness and mental activity. Their presentation will project confidence, without being overbearing or loud.

Class Presidents are more likely to make eye contact when engaged in individual conversation, unlike other, shyer Character Codes. To demonstrate that they have it together and controlled, they typically will not use a lot of hand gestures when they speak. They often appear serious because they are "in their heads" and thinking of the next task at hand.

From across the room, the Class President is not the one who is going to casually smile and glance your way. Why? Because he or she is busy either assessing the interpersonal dynamics in the room or thinking about some idea or problem—contemplating a new opportunity, working out a strategy, determining how to deal with an employee. Class Presidents are strategic thinkers, and they are always "on." They are typically competitive, alert, and innovative.

Class Presidents might seem rushed or preoccupied at times; this is because they are the quintessential multitaskers. Yet their focus is keen as a laser. If they decide to talk with someone at a meeting or cocktail party, they move very quickly, heading in a beeline toward that individual, intent on fulfilling their objective as quickly and efficiently as possible.

Speaking

Class Presidents prefer to converse and work with people who get to the point. They want to know the bottom line, now. When they speak, it is frank and direct; they frequently come across as demanding. They are often idea people and innovators. They are detail oriented and cerebral; theirs is the language of "I think" or "I see" more often than "I feel."

Class Presidents are problem solvers and troubleshooters. Ask them to take a look at something, and they'll rapidly fire off several possible solutions. You can tell when a Class President is on the other end of a phone call, because a Class President tends to end his or her sentences (and conversations) firmly and abruptly—unlike Cheerleaders, who tend to end sentences in a lilting, questioning manner.

Class Presidents and Texting

I have always liked to joke that it must have been a Class President that invented texting. Think about it. No need to pick up the phone. No need to say hello. No need to sign your name. Heck, you don't even need to use vowels.

Then one day I decided to research who actually *did* invent texting. I laughed out loud when I pulled up the photograph of the German inventor Freidheim Hillebrand. He's an engineer and technical writer and fits the Class President–Scholar Character Code!

And his comment about discovering that most questions were 160 characters or less that led to the invention of texting: "This is perfectly sufficient."

* * *

A Class President colleague and I decided to join forces to work on a fund-raising project to benefit the local schools. It was an event that would involve organizing many tasks and a lot of people. After an efficient meeting with the people in charge of the venue, we were both walking back out to our cars when she asked me, "So, we can just text and e-mail each other quick notes, right? No need to say 'Hello' or chat about the weather?" I laughed and replied, "Of course."

Our communication consisted of the quickest, smoothest, and most effective electronic conversations I've had, and the event was very successful!

Conducting business with Class Presidents means you need to be on your toes. If they are making an important decision, for example, deciding to purchase your product or contract for your services, they usually come to a quick and definitive decision, providing you know how to present your information in a clear, concise manner and meet their driving need for certainty. If you don't have their attention, you may find them multitasking or checking their appointment book, all the while murmuring "Uh-huh, uh-huh" toward you. Ask them if they understood your point, and they will promptly repeat back the last two sentences you spoke, verbatim. On the other hand, if you hesitate when asked a question, the Class President assumes you are unprepared or don't know what you are talking about.

The Silly Cup of Coffee

Contributed by Rebecca H. G.

The Class President side of me wants to make sure we get everything done that I set out to do, loves to be organized, makes lists, and wants to deliver value.

My husband is a Scholar, so when we are in a stressed state, it does get interesting.

In work mode, I tend to take charge and push everything (and everyone) to deliver the results promised, whether people feel like it or not, and I become less patient with any details not important to the bottom line.

My husband, however, tends to become more concerned about the details. He wants to make sure we are doing everything perfectly.

The first time we worked together, my husband asked if he could do anything to help. I said, "Yes, I left my coffee in the main conference room space, in the back," and asked, "Would you mind getting it for me so I can continue to prepare?"

He said, "Sure." Then he disappeared for a while and returned with no coffee and wanting more complete directions as to where my coffee could be located.

I explained again that it was in the back of the room, on the window ledge toward the middle of the space.

He then wanted further clarification: "Which back? When you face the door? When you face the back of the room as the presenter? When you first walk into the back where the tables are?"

At this point, the coffee was becoming less important to me, and I was becoming more concerned with getting the work done.

So I said, "Never mind; that's okay. I will get it later."

He became a little more insistent that he was trying to help me, and he just needed more information. I became a little stronger in stating that I didn't really need the coffee at that moment; I needed to focus.

He ended up feeling hurt and frustrated that I wouldn't give him the details needed to find the coffee to help me. I ended up frustrated because it was taking too much time and energy to get the silly cup of coffee; it was easier to just get it myself.

Psyche

The four driving needs that influence the majority of our decisions include *certainty*, *variety*, *significance*, and *connection*. When your client's driving need is met—for example, through your selling or marketing—you can expect a positive outcome.

Driving Need

Class Presidents have a driving need for *certainty*. These individuals want to be in control, or at least have the sense of being in control. As they are obviously task-oriented people, they are very good at getting things done. They can see the beginning, middle, and end of a project and want to know that it will be carried out correctly. Class Presidents are concerned with doing things right. As noted earlier, this can come from having been taught as a child that there is a specific or right way to approach a task. Whenever you are presenting to an audience of Class Presidents, make certain you are speaking directly and decisively to their driving need for certainty.

Character Traits

Class Presidents are goal oriented, and they are competitive and like to win. They may move quickly from one accomplishment to another without stopping to reflect on their achievements—or yours. They rarely celebrate their progress or list their victories. Instead, they constantly focus on the task ahead and the next goal to reach. They want to keep the ball rolling.

The Quick Read

I was raised by a Class President mom. When I first wrote the Character Code System, I asked her to read it. Now, mind you, the first draft outline was 125 pages.

I was more than a little miffed when she pulled a typical Class President move, flipping through the pages in about five seconds flat.

"Read it," I said, "I think it is really good, and I put a lot of work into it."

"I did. It's nice" was her reply.

Many months later she finally read the overview for just the Class President. Her response: "What did you do, just write down everything you knew about me?"

I laughed out loud! I love it when people read their Character Code and have that same response.

Now my mom is one of my biggest supporters and relays stories of how understanding the Character Codes has impacted her work and life. High praise from a Class President!

It goes without saying that Class Presidents are great managers. They can handle an ER trauma unit, conduct high-pressure legal negotiations, or sustain the multitasking required to launch a start-up or run a growing business.

They cut through red tape, office politics, or other peoples' issues to clarify problems and quickly resolve them. They prefer working under pressure and with tight deadlines. Class Presidents have a reputation for quickly finding solutions to any problem, but they may have trouble taking the time to praise coworkers and celebrate the victories along the way.

The Inner Meanie

The inner meanie is that negative voice in our head we all have. What it tells us depends on our Character Code. The Class President's inner meanie is constantly critical of him or her. In fact, this is the most judgmental of all the Character Codes because of this critical nature. Some have evolved past criticizing subordinates or situations, either verbally or mentally, but remain very critical of themselves.

In a healthy state, Class Presidents can be highly motivating. They can inspire others to action with the mantra "You can be anyone and do anything you set your mind to." Others may draw from the Class Presidents' power and strength. In an unhealthy state, their inner meanie comes from the feeling they are not right, not whole, not worthy, not good enough. Again, as noted previously, this can come from being constantly corrected as a child and taught that there was one specific way to approach each task.

We do not know which aspects of human behavior are genetic and which are formed from experience. However, it is clear that when discussing nature versus nurture, both play an important role. Regardless of how the driving need for certainty originated for the Class President, you will want to recognize the importance it plays in dictating the person's daily behavior.

Access the resource "Taming the Class President Meanie" for tips and insight (and a little humor) at http://charactercode.com/classpresidentmeanie.

Conflict, Stress, and Emotions

Class Presidents may experience feelings of jealousy or inadequacy regarding people and situations, although they rarely show those feelings. They are often too competitive, and they make the quickest judgment call of all the Character Codes. In healthy situations, they can be very reasonable and logical about letting go of an assumption once it has been proved wrong. However, in unhealthy situations, they may hold grudges and cling to their original assumptions. Forgiveness isn't their strong suit; how can they forgive others if they cannot forgive themselves? They usually give themselves or others too little wiggle room.

Class Presidents may be unaware of other people's Character Codes and expect others to be just like them. When they are aware of others' feelings, however, they are able to moderate their behavior appropriately. When frustrated, the Class President is typically impatient, even rude. Class Presidents often struggle with their sense of urgency and complain when others are, in their eyes, inept or slow.

Health and Wellness

Class Presidents push through life, including the aches, pains, and illnesses that come their way. As a result, they may experience health issues particularly later in life. Many of these issues are related to stress, because of the tough demands and high expectations they place upon themselves. This results from the disconnect between their bodies and their active minds. Often, the Class President body has to "scream out" in order to get any attention.

Of all the Character Codes, the Class President is the least likely to be a hypochondriac and is often too impatient to tolerate therapy or alternative health practices. Class Presidents may handle their car the same way they handle their body: they expect it to keep going with very little TLC.

If you work in healthcare and want to focus on Class Presidents as clients, be aware that many will want you to just fix the immediate problem and will want to forgo committing to a process of healing themselves. In that case, you need to explain that working at such a high mental level is consuming physical resources at an equally high level. They must understand that only by committing to a health-centered regimen will they be able to sustain their work level and lifestyle. Without tying your health recommendations to their productivity, the Class President patient will just have an attitude of "get in and get out"—often waiting too long to seek treatment.

Jobs and Careers

Class Presidents gravitate to demanding jobs, which explains why many business owners and world leaders are Class Presidents. Class Presidents are generally successful due to their drive, determination, self-motivation, ability to multitask, and time management skills. They have financially rewarding jobs or careers, often at the executive level, in such fields as finance, real estate, banking, upper-level healthcare, medicine, and consulting. Many successful entrepreneurs are Class Presidents as well, because they crave the demands and satisfactions of being their own boss.

Class Presidents must take care to strike a balance between the need to succeed and time spent with their family. These high-powered, highly focused businesspeople are often unaware of how quickly time passes and may look back with regret in later years when thinking of their 14- to 18-hour workdays.

Marketing and Sales

When marketing to a Class President, be sure your look is clean and corporate and that your message conveys competence, trust, and success. Pay careful consideration to your personal appearance, presentation, and speaking style, as well as your online presence: headshot, website, colors, and titles. Colors that appeal to the Class President include blue, black, gray, brown, white, and sometimes a jewel color (although it is not preferred). Avoid pastels, as well as anything too flamboyant or busy.

If you want to market and sell to Class Presidents, consider what problems you can help them to solve. Don't spend time creating a product, service, or program for a Class President that focuses on a skill they already have mastered. Use what you've learned in this chapter to focus on the skills they lack if you want to serve them. The Class President will appreciate the fact that you're well prepared and haven't wasted his or her time, and will respond in kind with a quick, definitive decision. Tailor your presentation to appeal to the Class President's Character Code, as discussed in the next section.

The Ideal Client

If the Class President is your ideal client, it is essential that you make an absolutely fabulous first impression that inspires trustworthiness and success. You must offer assurances that you are highly competent and organized, you are totally committed to your Class President client's success, and your product or service will meet and exceed all expectations. Although everyone values a first impression, it is always a make-or-break situation with the Class President.

It is useful to know that Class Presidents prefer to be around other Class Presidents more than any other Character Code. If you are not a Class President by nature, you need to be aware of how Class Presidents think if they're your ideal client. Always remember, if you hesitate, seem unsure, or waver at all in discussing your work or solution with a Class President, he or she will assume you do not know what you are talking about.

Summarizing the Class President

If you are a Class President, or it is one of your top two Character Codes, then you can start by being more tolerant toward yourself. When you notice the inner meanie criticizing how you look, what you did, or where your path is headed, remind yourself this is just a part of being a Class President. Tell the inner meanie to take the night off. Of course you are headed in the right direction. You are fine just the way you are.

Advice for the Class President

If you are a Class President and feel impatient or frustrated with others, remind yourself that this is just a feeling and a part of being a

Class President. Every Character Code is different, but each has just as much inherent value as any other. You, as a leader, must learn to appreciate the differences and use them to good advantage. This is why I like teaching the Character Code System: it helps Character Codes become a more brilliant version of themselves and more tolerant of everyone else.

As a Class President you are inherently very quick. Once you know and understand all the Character Codes, you will be able to apply your newfound understanding and begin treating people in a gentler, more respectful manner. This will only increase the number of clients who will want to benefit from your powerful leadership skills and help them drive toward success. You'll see ever-better results interacting with the public at large, and in a word, you'll become unstoppable.

Advice for Interacting with Class Presidents

If you aren't a Class President but your ideal client is, you need to consider the visual and verbal messages you send for effectively communicating with him or her. Class Presidents want to know you are trustworthy and will get the job done. For example, if they have outsourced a job to you, they trust that you know your process and can complete the task, but they don't need to know every minute detail of your progress. What they care about the most is that you get it done.

Review the earlier "Appearance," "Presentation," and "Speaking" sections. How can you apply some of those attributes to yourself in order to more effectively connect with the Class President? I'm not talking about an extreme makeover; rather, subtle things that tell the Class President you are his or her type of colleague. Class Presidents make the quickest assumptions. They prefer being around people of their own Character Code; however, they will respect the "shiny" or professional version of you as your own Character Code. Always honor who you are and make the effort to make sure your message connects with your audience.

Think through if the Class President is the ideal client for you. If yes, you'll need to make sure your competence is clearly known. Can you accept someone who is direct, and can you take orders? If you are looking for a warm and fuzzy client, then the Class President might not be the right fit. You always get to decide which ideal client you most desire to work with. You don't need to be the same Character Code or have the same driving need, but if you do select a different Character Code as your ideal client, you will want to make sure you understand how to serve that client.

First Impressions with the Class President

When meeting a Class President for the first time, be sure you look pulled together and appear confident. Move in a quick, decisive manner. Shake hands firmly, with one pump, and make eye contact. Class Presidents prefer business language to emotional or spiritual language. Use concrete, businesslike language—for example, *target market* instead of *dream customer.*

Here are some things you can do to enhance your first impression that broadcasts *trustworthy* to a Class President:

>> Wear a strand of pearls or moderate, classic jewelry.

>> Make sure your hair is neat.

>> Choose classic lines in clothing, not too dramatic or natural in color or style.

>> Radiate an overall polished and professional look.

>> Keep your eyes alert, paying attention to details in the environment.

>> Use direct language with tangible details of what you offer and can accomplish.

Here are some aspects that send a warning or spell out danger to a Class President and should be avoided:

>> You're not wearing any jewelry or just very little, indicating you didn't put any effort into your look.

>> Your hair or clothing looks disheveled or too casual.

>> You're juggling too much stuff, or papers are strewn everywhere.

>> You appear sloppy or disorganized.

>> You don't make direct eye contact or are timidly looking down all the time.

>> You seem hesitant, take too long to answer, appear vague or nervous.

People respond differently to someone who is obviously nervous. An Activist Character Code would nurture you through it. A Cheerleader Character Code would tell you not to worry or tell you a joke to put you at ease. Class Presidents will likely assume you have a reason to be nervous and are not prepared. In other words, they will believe you and take at face value what they see before them.

One of the Class President's greatest strengths is being able to handle nearly any situation. That's why Class Presidents make great managers and leaders. You can count on them to do what they say they will do. They will take exceptional care of a project assignment from beginning to end. They follow up and follow through. They are very strategically minded and superbly visionary, capable of seeing the big picture and realizing grand dreams.

How to Read a Client Now

Now that you have read the Class President Character Code in detail, you'll want to remember to:

>> Begin your "people watching" with new eyes and see how many Class Presidents you can find.

>> Notice how the driving need for certainty dictates the Class President's behavior and appearance and start identifying the patterns you see.

>> Consider if the Class President is the right ideal Character Code client for you.

>> Observe what, if any, changes you would need to make in your personal branding to make sure you can communicate with the Class President.

>> Begin to feel more compassion for Class Presidents (or yourself) when you consider their inner meanie and what you learned in the "Psyche" section.

In Chapter 4 you will learn how to identify a Cheerleader Character Code. This will include all the details you need to better communicate with, connect to, attract, and read Cheerleaders from across the room.

Take the following action steps now:

>> Download the "Class President Character Code Overview" to have the details and color sketches right at your fingertips at http://charactercode.com/classpresident.

>> Access the resource "Taming the Class President Meanie" for tips and insight (and a little humor) at http://charactercode.com/classpresidentmeanie.

FOUR

The Cheerleader Character Code

I Just Want to Have Fun

THE CHEERLEADERS ARE so named because they care about having fun, are positive, bubbly, and friendly, and may seem like the "boy or girl next door." Cheerleader women are often very feminine, and Cheerleader men are often referred to as "metrosexual."

The Cheerleader's driving need is for variety. Cheerleaders are very people oriented and sociable and are natural communicators. They like excitement and the newness of an adventure or activity. They are great motivators, and just like their name, they can be very encouraging. Cheerleaders tend to show more emotion, are often inspirational, and can perform on a dime. All these characteristics suggest the Cheerleader's desire to feel alive and fear of being bored.

Are you a Cheerleader? Do you know people who are Cheerleaders? Now, using the three components of the first impression described in Chapter 1—appearance, presentation, and speaking style—here is how to read a Cheerleader from across the room.

Appearance

Your appearance is the most important aspect of your first impression. Those things we care most about are reflected in our appearance, and so we are constantly giving clues to others about how we want to be treated.

Hair

The Cheerleader woman most often has long or shoulder-length hair that is wavy or bouncy. This is the Character Code most likely to use a curling iron.

For some women in America, weight can influence their hair length, because so many believe (needlessly) they should wear short hair if they are heavy. As a result, some Cheerleader women who prefer a longer hairstyle may elect to wear it short due to weight. If so, they will typically have short hair with more body to the style. The Cheerleader will not wear a severe cut or a style that is too short or spiky.

She is the Character Code most likely to pull her hair up into a pony-tail, and typically she's the one as an adult who would dare wear pigtails because it's fun and cute. She may also wear barrettes or cute clips in her hair and is most likely to use headbands or a scarf in her hair.

The Cheerleader man typically has a hairstyle with body or wave to it and often uses hair products. You will see a lot of male celebrities sporting this tousled hairstyle. Other male Cheerleaders will wear the surfer look, but not past their chin.

Cheerleader men are typically clean shaven.

Makeup

The Cheerleader Character Code woman usually wears full makeup including some type of foundation or powder, eye makeup, lipstick, and often blush. She may experiment with more color than the Class President Character Code, but she is still tasteful in her choices. Her overall appearance is well made up—the girl next door—and rarely garish or overdone. She may lean more toward pastels or follow current fashion trends.

The Cheerleader male typically will not wear any makeup outside of stage makeup for media appearances.

Jewelry

The Cheerleader woman typically wears jewelry that is romantic in style and very feminine. She may wear items that range from dainty to a more layered look. Her necklaces are often multitiered and have charms or long strands. Beads, glass, flowers, and ribbon in jewelry indicate a Cheerleader Character Code.

If the Cheerleader wears pearls, it will be a more romantic version, including several strands or perhaps colored pearls. Her jewelry selection reflects that she is more interested in looking pretty and feminine than powerful.

The male Cheerleader may wear a silver or gold bracelet or neck-lace. His wedding band is more likely to have diamonds or be more stylish than a traditional gold band. If suits are required for work, he may choose to sport cuff links and have a number of styles. His watch will range from a trendy multifunctional sports watch to a brand-name dress watch.

Clothing

The Cheerleader Character Code often expresses variety in clothing as well as in life. He or she may select pastels and likes to wear color. Think of women's blouses and men's dress shirts. Cheerleader men and women like to appear fashionable and may covet designer-label clothing or follow the latest trends.

Some Cheerleader women may wear black—for example, if they feel they're overweight—reflecting the common belief that wearing black makes you look thin. If you identify yourself as a Cheerleader Character Code wanting to wear color but feel trapped into wearing black to look trim, I suggest you wear your color and just go with a monochromatic look. Wearing the same color or shade of color can be just as slimming while allowing you to express your personality.

The Cheerleader woman often selects more feminine clothing that is light and airy with ruffles and floral prints that are girly, flirty, and fun. She may show a little more skin, but she will still be tasteful and conservative. The Cheerleader woman is also more likely to wear skirts or dresses than other Character Codes.

Cheerleader men who dress up will often wear a pastel dress shirt with contrasting colors in their tie. They are often described as a clothes horse and are very stylish in their appearance. Whether dressed up or casual, they look pulled together.

For a casual look you can still expect both Cheerleader men and women to be color coordinated and retain that boy- or girl-next-door appearance. Overall they present as well-dressed, friendly, and approachable.

Accessories

The Cheerleader woman is more likely to have a pretty purse than something simply functional. Her purse has feminine touches or color. She's turned off by a black briefcase. Cheerleaders often love the type of bags that have one interior and interchangeable outside shells. This appeals to the Cheerleader because she is fashionable and appreciates bags that are aesthetically pleasing. She may also like brand names and labels. One trendy Cheerleader choice would be the bags with the large multilayered flower on the face that takes up the whole side of the purse.

Don't Scare Them Away

I once attended a two day event and had no idea who my audience was when I walked in.

I showed up in my typical Class President gear and looked like an uptight, straight laced woman all in black.

Turns out the whole room was filled with Cheerleaders and Activists.

On the first day, no one approached me or talked to me.

On day two I switched it up, added some color and some accessories that were more "friendly" for the crowd.

The results were telling as I lost count of how many people came up to compliment me on my necklace and thus began a conversation . . . and a connection.

Cheerleader men likely carry a stylish briefcase or occasionally a trendy man bag worn over the opposite shoulder. You will also see Cheerleader men carrying stylish bags or cases for their iPads or laptops. Where the classic black briefcase may be expected, Cheerleader men will tote briefcases in tan or brown, even mahogany or maroon, with rounded corners or over-the-top flaps representing their sense of fashion.

Nails

Cheerleader Character Code women often wear their nails longer (past their fingertips) and use a color. The most common colors are shades of pink, but they are typically conservative in their choices, preferring pretty over shocking. Some like a French manicure, which often indicates a Class President and Cheerleader combination.

The Cheerleader woman is also likely to have colored, manicured toenails and enjoys a mani-pedi outing with her girlfriends. In contrast, the Class President is most likely to schedule an appointment by herself to get it off her to-do list, whereas the Cheerleader considers it a fun event made even better when with a friend.

Cheerleader men represent the Character Code mostly likely to get a manicure. When you see a man with clear polish or buffed nails, he is probably a Cheerleader. Along with the Actor, the Cheerleader is the male Character Code most likely to spend time in a spa or salon receiving treatments, including facials and manicures.

Shoes

Cheerleader women often wear pumps or heels for business in a variety of styles or colors. They may wear a fashionable nude heel or a trendy ballet-style dress shoe. The Cheerleader is also the Character Code most likely to wear cute sandals and could easily compete with the Actor and Artist Character Codes for who has the most shoes!

Cheerleader men are likely to wear stylish shoes like a trendy dress shoe such as a European oxford. You'll also see them in fashion tennis shoes or top siders. A male Cheerleader keeps his shoes in good repair and well polished. He owns more pairs of shoes than many of the other men and may rotate styles daily.

Presentation

The presentation style of the Cheerleader Character Code reflects an outgoing attitude and a desire for fun. Cheerleader women love to project feminine energy and exuberance, while Cheerleader men are upbeat and friendly.

Cheerleaders are more likely to punctuate their conversations with laughter, giggles, and smiles. They can be flirty and fun in how they carry themselves. You will often notice Cheerleader men and women lightly rest their hands on people as they speak to them. Cheerleaders are typically more fluid in their body posture and the most likely to link arms with others or put their arm across another's shoulders. They can be huggers. From across the room, Cheerleaders are the ones flitting from person to person or group to group.

Cheerleaders are good at making eye contact, but they are easily distracted by other people or activities around them. They might be focused on the conversation and then suddenly exclaim, "Oh, there's a squirrel!" Bright, shiny objects will divert their attention.

Kinder to Myself

Contributed by Victoria B.

Before I knew about the Character Code System, I used to be really hard on myself. I could not understand why I would be working on a project and walk into a room to get something for that project, and the next thing I knew I would be rearranging the books on my shelf.

I was also famous for sitting down at the computer to write an e-mail for a pressing situation and two minutes later find myself gathering new friends on Facebook. What was up with that?

When I realized that I am a Cheerleader, and one of the challenges is that we get distracted easily, I felt this sense of relief. I never knew that so many people had the same problem that I had; I thought I was the only one!

Knowing that I need variety, I can now plan my day to include multiple projects and different tasks within those projects.

I still have to work on staying focused, but now that I am aware of it, it seems to come easier. The greatest benefit of knowing about Character Coding is the awareness that you get about your own habits and patterns.

Cheerleaders use enthusiastic hand gestures in conversation. If you shake hands, they might continue shaking yours up and down while talking at the same time, or they might do a double-clasp handshake. Sometimes you may see a Cheerleader across a room who appears rushed, as if he or she has a lot going on and is trying to juggle it all. If the Cheerleader feels overwhelmed, he or she will show it, whereas the Class President would try to hide it. Cheerleaders tend to be more emotional and freely express their feelings on their faces and in their body posture, whether happy (most common), sad, angry, confused, or bored.

Speaking

The Cheerleader Character Code is a talker and often a blurter. Cheerleaders will typically interrupt—not because they want to be rude, but because an idea or thought just crossed their mind and they're excited to share it. They like connecting with people, and talking is their most common way to do that.

Cheerleaders are the most likely to notice someone else's appearance and make a positive comment, such as "I like your necklace," or "You have such pretty hair," or "That's a great jacket. Where did you get it?" They are often good at making small talk or starting a conversation with strangers.

Cheerleaders can be funny and are likely to share a story or a joke. You will often notice them laughing and surrounded by people. Because they are such excited talkers, they may sometimes come across as argumentative. They can be very persuasive and convincing in their conversation and passionate in their verbal expression. As a result, they are often quite inspirational and lean toward optimism. Many motivational speakers are Cheerleaders.

The tone of a Cheerleader's speech is typically upbeat and quite often has real emotion behind it. Cheerleaders frequently have a lift or lilt at the ends of their sentences. Cheerleaders speak in friendly, personable, and casual language. They rarely use formal speech patterns and sometimes share too much personal information.

Psyche

The four driving needs that influence the majority of our decisions include *certainty, variety, significance,* and *connection.* When your client's driving need is met—for example, through your selling or marketing—you can expect a positive outcome.

Driving Need

Cheerleaders are driven by an inner desire to make things fun and exciting. Their driving need is variety. They like to be entertained and to be entertaining, and they enjoy making others laugh. This can come from having received feedback as a child that life is good when you are happy and positive. Cheerleader children were often in plays, dance recitals, or choruses, where they received applause—which they may still crave as adults through work or by performing good deeds. Some Cheerleader children were the class clowns and liked the attention and response they received by keeping their peers entertained.

A boring or lonely life is one of their fears. Because of this driving need for variety, Cheerleaders may find themselves jumping from project to project. They need to develop concentration skills to stay on task or complete the job. They suffer from getting bored easily and losing interest quickly; couple that with a desire to be liked, and the result is that they often say yes to too many things or too many people.

Character Traits

Cheerleaders are fast paced and persuasive. They are often great speakers and can handle impromptu presentations and toasts or respond quickly in a pinch. Cheerleaders enjoy accomplishing goals, but it's the experience along the way of attaining those goals fueled by the anticipated recognition that interests them the most. When they win, they celebrate.

For Cheerleaders, any event is better if they have someone with whom to attend it and share the experience. For a Cheerleader, that means talking and commenting. Anyone who has ever sat next to someone who talked or whispered through an entire event sat next to a Cheerleader.

The Cheerleader is a positive motivator with quick ideas who can inspire others. An overzealous Cheerleader can seem "salesy" or phony.

Cheerleaders are joiners and leaders and like to know what is going on. Because their number one way of relating to someone is through conversation, they must be careful not to gossip. Other people's problems interest them, and so this Character Code is the most likely to enjoy soap operas.

Cheerleaders like to share stories and really appreciate personal information about the people they deal with in business (the Class President does not). Cheerleaders may exaggerate for the sake of a good story or just to keep themselves entertained.

If the Cheerleader woman watches baseball, it is likely she will care about the story behind the pitcher and his wife and kids, but it is unlikely she will know his earned-run average. The Cheerleader man will like the camaraderie of watching sports with a friend and prefer the social aspect of enjoying the event.

In a healthy state, the Cheerleader can be very motivating and supportive of others and will build them up. Others may feed off their energy and enthusiasm. They can make work fun. The character Tom Sawyer was a Cheerleader, convincing other kids to paint the fence for him.

The Inner Meanie

For Cheerleaders, the inner meanie is one that tells them they're not important. Depending on their ability to deal with this, they may be really suffering with trying to prove they are needed as they seek validation from others.

Cheerleaders often base their sense of inner safety on feedback received from the outer world. This tenuous basis for self-worth often dictates a much-needed inward journey of discovery at some point in the Cheerleader's life.

Cheerleaders want their accomplishments noticed. Whereas Class Presidents will accomplish things because they like to do things right and are competitive with themselves, Cheerleaders like to accomplish things to get a positive reaction and recognition from those around them.

Access the resource "Taming the Cheerleader Meanie" for tips and insight (and a little humor) at http://charactercode.com/cheerleadermeanie.

Conflict, Stress, and Emotions

One of the reasons Cheerleaders seek the approval and praise of others, struggling with the ability to say no, is because they don't want to offend or upset anyone. They do not like confrontation. As a result, Cheerleaders often do too much and say yes too often, which can create a crisis in their lives as they can become prone to being overwhelmed.

Cheerleaders are usually very open and very honest, of course, operating from their own perspective, which they typically take as complete fact. Sometimes Cheerleaders are naive or may overshare, which can lead to embarrassing situations at best or really devastated feelings in some scenarios.

In an unbalanced situation, Cheerleaders may be argumentative and get angry and defensive easily. They can be very attached to their opinions, and emotions will run high. In a balanced situation, they will have level emotions and consider the perspectives of others. Cheerleaders are typically good at letting you know how they feel, which isn't always appreciated by the other Character Codes.

Cheerleaders can be effective in diffusing some tough situations and turning them around in a more positive direction. However, because they don't like confrontation, they may be too quick to gloss over issues and paint a rosy picture. In a state of awareness, the Cheerleader can be sensitive to other people's different Character Codes and make each person feel really good about themselves.

Due to the desire of Cheerleaders to have fun and keep things lighthearted, they don't appreciate difficult tasks and may react in anger, impatience, or frustration.

Cheerleader in Graduate School

As a Class President with some Cheerleader, I get a double dose of the fun (and challenges) from each Character Code. I distinctly remember experiencing the Cheerleader frustration when faced with difficult tasks throughout my education.

I was earning my honors degree in communications from Loyola Marymount University, and the "benefit" of the Honors College was having my courses taught by PhDs, which meant diving deeper into every subject. I was doing fine until it came to history. I probably belonged in remedial history—it was my worst subject—but I was required to take the advanced course.

I hired a fellow student to take notes for me so that I could just sit in class and totally focus on the teacher. If I had a single "squirrel" moment and zoned for a minute, it was like missing decades of world history. I sat in the back of the classroom, talked to no one, and did my best to focus and grasp the history of the world. I thought I was quietly anonymous.

I only missed one day of that class. A classmate later told me that in the middle of the lecture the professor paused mid-sentence and said, "You know, Brandy doesn't think I notice that she isn't here today—but I do because I don't feel that 'buzzzzzz' from the back of the room."

Apparently my Cheerleader angst and attempt to focus was so intense it was noticed by the professor in a packed classroom—even from the back of the room!

* * *

I had a similar experience later in life. I thought I was done with school but decided to return and earn my doctorate of chiropractic degree. Since I had a bachelor of arts, this meant diving into the world of science for the first time in my life.

I was required to take biochemistry, physics, biology, and every anatomy and pathology course you could imagine. What's more, I was handed my schedule of courses by the college each quarter and didn't have any say in which classes to take or how many.

I admit, I was stressed and angry for the first several weeks of each quarter. I would feel overwhelmed and think, "How do they expect a human to take 35 hours of science each week?" Of course, it was doable—I just never felt that in the beginning. My Cheerleader was challenged, and I would react in frustration. Those poor teachers!

When you know this about yourself, you can manage it and keep it in perspective. Even better is to use the energy and emotion to fuel the results you want. I ended up graduating second in my class and magna cum laude. If only we could know the end result when we first start.

Health and Wellness

Healthwise, Cheerleaders will struggle with any type of routine, whether the demand is to consistently take vitamins, work out, keep a series of appointments, and so on. They may initially be very enthusiastic, but their interest will wane, especially if the reason they started has gone away, such as pain. This is really important for those of you that are health practitioners, speakers, coaches, entrepreneurs, or executives marketing in the health and wellness field. If your ideal client is a Cheerleader and you have some type of regimen to be followed, this can be a frustrating battle. The Cheerleader is the Character Code most likely to quit a project or back out of a commitment.

If you do work in the health and wellness field and have some type of regimen for Cheerleaders to follow, you will need to make it fun and remind them of the benefits. If you can create a social aspect that will add interest for Cheerleaders, it will be even more effective.

Cheerleaders will also lean toward emotion, drama, and hyperbole regarding health concerns. Their emotions will run the gamut from excessive worry as they fear the worst to an endless optimism and naiveté as they hope for the best.

Jobs and Careers

Many Cheerleaders become salespeople, performers, and public speakers, largely in response to the high energy and entertainment demands of those jobs. There is also a certain degree of flexibility and opportunity to be creative that appeals to their driving need for variety. They often love the travel involved and the opportunity to be recognized or receive kudos from the crowd.

Though many Cheerleaders are successful, they may struggle with systems and organization in their work. The Cheerleader can easily get off topic or go on a tangent, which can be challenging in some work situations.

The area that Cheerleaders have to be careful with is making decisions too quickly and managing their professional reputation so that they are able to provide good customer service, follow-through, and reliability. If they do too much or grow too fast, they set themselves up for getting overwhelmed and burned out and may quit. Like most of us, the key is to find a balance that allows you to play to your Character Code strengths—magnifying your skill set and seeking support for your challenges.

Marketing and Sales

When it comes to making a purchase or deciding to become your client, Cheerleaders definitely get caught up in the feeling, strongly buy on emotion, and place huge weight on their intuition and gut feelings.

They also like to move fast but may commit to something and change their mind later. This can happen because they got caught up in the excitement initially but don't feel the same later or because they said yes to too many things.

Cheerleaders' dreams may involve making fantasy appearances on Oprah or accepting an Oscar. They envision and crave recognition.

Their greatest fear is to be alone or lonely without anyone to connect with, as they feed off the company and response of others. Cheerleaders' nightmares usually involve thinking no one likes them, being alone, being bored, or having nothing to do.

It is very important for Cheerleaders that are senior citizens to have an active lifestyle for good mental health. Entrepreneurs that cater to the over-50 crowd, depending on the topic, might find Cheerleaders an ideal client, as they won't be content just sitting at home like some other senior Character Codes.

When marketing to a Cheerleader, pay careful consideration to your headshot, website, colors, and titles. Good colors for a Cheerleader would be bright and vibrant. Avoid earthy neutrals and anything boring or too basic. Make sure your message is high energy and fun.

Read through this section many times, and you will see what problems the Cheerleader needs solved. For example, you could solve problems that help the Cheerleader manage time more efficiently, become organized, avoid feeling overwhelmed, and getting things completed as related to your business offers.

The Ideal Client

If the Cheerleader is your ideal client, it is essential that you make a first impression that shows you are fun to work with. You will then need to build in systems to handle follow-up, as you may spend more time chasing these clients after they have committed to you. It isn't that they are ignoring you or are uninterested; it's just that they have committed to so many things, and Cheerleaders are really top-of-mind people, meaning whatever is in front of them gets their attention. A Cheerleader appreciates reminder calls and e-mails for all scheduled appointments.

Because the Cheerleader is so spontaneous and impulsive, make sure that you are clear about your refund policies and that you really present the benefits of your program. I believe the three-day buyer's remorse law in California was created just for Cheerleaders!

However, when you do a job well and the Cheerleader is pleased, he or she will tell everyone about you! One or two good Cheerleader clients could provide a huge amount of referrals for your business.

Cheerleaders prefer to be around other Cheerleaders more than any other type of Character Code. They also get along with Activists and some Actors. They're the least compatible with Scholars.

Summarizing the Cheerleader

If you are a Cheerleader, or it is one of your top two Character Codes, you can start by being more tolerant toward yourself. When you notice that inner meanie suggesting you aren't important or don't matter, remind yourself that this meanie is just part of being a Cheerleader. Tell the meanie to take the night off. Of course you matter. Everyone matters. No proof is required.

Advice for the Cheerleader

When you feel angry, frustrated, impatient, or bored with others or some situation, remind yourself this is just a feeling. You don't have to be entertained every minute of the day. Sometimes it is important to just be still. Value can be found in the moment.

As a Cheerleader, when you know all the Codes, you can apply that information and use your influence and powers of persuasion to build up the other Character Codes. With these skills, you will attract all types of people to you like a magnet. You will be a force of nature in your social interactions.

Advice for Interacting with Cheerleaders

If you aren't a Cheerleader but your ideal client is one, you need to consider the visual and verbal messaging you must send in order to effectively communicate. A Cheerleader wants to know you are fun to work with. This is especially important if you work in an area that can be a little dry or is very detailed. I suggest using humor and visual aids and engaging your audience.

Review the "Appearance," "Presentation," and "Speaking" sections of the Cheerleader and consider adding some of those items to your look and behavior in order to connect with the Cheerleader crowd. Remember, though, always be true to who you are and see what little things you can add to make your ideal client comfortable.

This isn't about getting into costume. Rather, it is about honoring who you are and making sure your message rings true for your audience.

Remember, too, Cheerleaders like things to be aesthetically pleasing. If you want to enhance their acceptance of your presentation materials, make sure to use a handsome or pretty binder rather than a plain manila file folder. And don't bore them with mind-boggling details. Make sure you know that the Cheerleader is the proper ideal client for you and that you have effective systems in place. If it seems things are not working well, perhaps the Cheerleader is not your ideal client. The alternative is choosing a different client who is more connected to you or compatible with your business. This is something I evaluate in great detail with my private consulting clients.

First Impressions with the Cheerleader

When meeting a Cheerleader for the first time, be sure you look friendly and pulled together. Move toward Cheerleaders in a confident and open manner, shake hands or hug, and look into their eyes and smile. Looking slick or closed down is a turnoff.

Cheerleaders often prefer feeling and personal language to business language. For example, using morals or values to describe someone's character is more appealing than talking about life skills or life lessons. Speak in terms of your ideal client or dream client rather than your target market.

Here are some things you can do to enhance your first impression that broadcasts fun to a Cheerleader:

>> Choose pretty jewelry with a little flair, maybe whimsical, just not too dramatic.
>> Wear flowing hair, shoulder length.
>> Dress in a flirty skirt or jacket or shirt with ruffles (not tuxedo style).
>> Look nicely dressed, but not too businesslike.
>> Make eye contact; look excited and alive.
>> Speak openly, share your feelings, and have dreams and ideas.

Here are some aspects that send a warning or spell out danger to a Cheerleader and should be avoided:

>> You look flawless, with everything done perfectly.

>> You carry an intimidating and large briefcase or are sporting a pocket protector.

>> You never smile.

>> You seem too bossy, too organized, too rigid, or too specific, and you lack spontaneity.

One of the Cheerleader's greatest strengths is being able to turn a negative situation into a positive one and encouraging others. That's why Cheerleaders often make great business partners or strategic alliances. You can count on them to have good public relations skills and the ability to speak effectively and be motivational. They are dreamers and see the big picture; however, you will need to help them manage the details.

How to Read a Client Now

Now that you have read the Cheerleader Character Code in detail, you'll want to remember to:

» Begin your "people watching" with new eyes and see how many Cheerleaders you can find.

» Notice how the driving need for variety dictates the Cheerleader's behavior and appearance and start identifying the patterns you see.

» Consider if the Cheerleader is the right ideal Character Code client for you.

» Observe what, if any, changes you would need to make in your personal branding to make sure you can communicate with the Cheerleader.

» Begin to feel more compassion for Cheerleaders (or yourself) when you consider what you know about their inner meanie and what you learned in the "Psyche" section.

In Chapter 5 you will learn how to identify an Actor Character Code. This will include all the details you need to better communicate with, connect to, attract, and read Actors from across the room.

Take the following action steps now:

» Download the "Cheerleader Character Code Overview" to have the details and color sketches right at your fingertips at http://charactercode.com/cheerleader.

» Access the resource "Taming the Cheerleader Meanie" for tips and insight (and a little humor) at http://charactercode.com/cheerleadermeanie.

FIVE

The Actor Character Code

Bigger, Bolder, Better

T HE ACTOR LOVES to project power and high energy all rolled into one fabulous package often described as *bigger*, *bolder*, and *better*. The Actor can demonstrate a wide variety of character traits, a penchant for expressing powerful emotion, and a driving need for significance.

Actors have a big personality and can swing their focus from people to tasks, depending on their current mood. They move fast, laugh loud, and are often misunderstood by the other Character Codes.

Can you envision some Actors you know? Are you an Actor? I'll break down the aura of the Actor into sections so that you have a clear idea of how to identify the Actor in a crowd. Here is how to read an Actor from across the room.

Appearance

Remember, the things we care about most are reflected in our appearance, which constantly gives clues to others about how we want to be treated.

Hair

You can often spot Actors a mile away based on the person's full and big head of hair. This is typically untamed for men, big and styled for women. I have teased some of my Actress clients that their hair is "one can of hairspray short of Texas." If their hair is short, it will often have volume and height. If long, it is full and may be wavy or curly.

That need for significance will show up in their appearance. Rarely will you see a boring or subdued hair style on Actors, unless they're making up for this mundane look another way, such as with dramatic clothing or jewelry.

Hair for both Actor men and women will be noticeable based on volume, creative styling, or use of color, extensions, or hair accessories.

Actor men are often clean shaven but occasionally sport the latest trends in moustache or beard (typically little more than a 5 p.m. shadow). The deciding factor is that it adds to their sexy look so that they are seen.

Makeup

Actresses definitely wear full makeup, usually the most of all the Character Codes. They may elect to wear an "evening look" during the day and can be extreme with color choices. They rarely are seen without being made up.

Actresses often choose brighter lip color or may wear red lipstick. Some vary from wearing merely dramatic makeup to what is often termed as garish by other Character Codes.

Men who wear eyeliner may be an Actor or an Artist Character Code.

Jewelry

Actresses' jewelry will range from classic to romantic to natural in style; regardless, it will typically be dramatic. They often select big, eye-catching items. They may choose large pendants or large earrings. The Actress typically wears the most jewelry of all the Character Codes. She is the most likely to wear multiple rings and bracelets or a lot of sparkle or "bling."

If you see men wearing sparkly jewelry or lots of diamonds, they're Actors. They will rarely wear a necktie without a conspicuous tie clip or some other showy jewelry item or accessory. You may see them wearing jeweled cuff links when formal dress is required or large diamond stud earrings even in casual dress mode. And no Actor will have a boring-looking watch. Be it expensive or not, you will notice it, often along with an unusual or unique ring.

Clothing

The Actress loves color—bright clothing or large floral prints. When wearing black, it may be a bold black-and-white geometric pattern or all black with bright accessories and jewelry. The Actress may overdo the animal prints, and is the most likely to have a sexy look or show too much cleavage. In business, she has to be careful about this.

Actor men are known for wearing bright-colored dress shirts, large and loud Hawaiian shirts, and wild ties. Whether it be a powerful suit, a sultry shirt, or a bright jersey, it will most likely be over the top. An Actor might also wear a stylish light scarf around his jacket—clear evidence of his need for significance. If a man walks into a party sporting that rare hat, it is a good bet that he is an Actor or Artist Character Code. If the look shouts out "I want to be noticed," then it is the Actor; whereas if the look is more artsy or vintage, then it is the Artist.

Accessories

The Actress is the most likely of all the Character Codes to carry a very large purse or bag that is often just as dramatic as she is. She'll use anything from bright colors to animal prints, with jewelry or scarves hanging from her purse. This is the one Character Code that would carry a pink animal-print bag.

Male Actors usually don't carry any type of bag or briefcase, as they don't want to be encumbered. They would prefer to have an assistant carry their items. If they do need to carry something, it is more likely to be the newest iPad or pricey tech gadget with a custom-designed cover that includes their logo or image.

Nails

Actresses tend to wear their nails longer and brighter than other Character Codes. Actresses may have a painted design, painted pattern, or rhinestones on their nails. This is one of the ways to quickly identify an Actress in uniform, as she may be forced to dress in the status quo but display a very decorative nail.

Like the Cheerleader, the Actress would consider a trip to the salon not only a fun activity, but a grooming necessity.

The male Actor will be well manicured, to be sure, and might apply a light buff to his nails.

Shoes

The Actress loves wearing shoes with a dramatic heel. Her shoes range from stilettos to high-heeled boots and from animal prints to flourishes, beads, or bows. You name it, and it's a viable option for the Actress.

Actor men may wear brightly colored high-tops, fancy dress shoes, snakeskin boots, or other stylized shoes.

Both Actor men and women are likely to own multiple pairs of shoes and enjoy shopping for the latest trends and styles.

The Actor look is definitely the *loudest* of all the Character Codes, and Actors will always appear to have the most fun. Actors are always noticeable in a room, but they have to be careful that their projected aura is for the right reasons, especially in business.

Presentation

Presentation is how you carry yourself—your posture, hand gestures, eye contact, facial expressions, movement, pacing, and the energy or telling vibe you emit as a person. You can recognize Actors by the way they hold themselves: they are commanding in their body posture. They range from appearing as the leader to appearing cocky or showing bravado.

Actors move fast and laugh loudly. In fact, they are called Actors because they express their emotions in such an emphatic way. They are the Character Code most animated in their facial expressions. If you ever see an adult making faces, he or she is probably an Actor.

As you'll read in the "Psyche" section, many Actors survived challenging childhoods that contributed to their strong personality traits. A good way to describe them is as cunning—capable of surviving on their own and making things happen. You'll see this in their presentation. A history of having to look out for "number one," be opportunistic, and make quick judgments about others is demonstrated in their body language and movement.

Don't be surprised if they quickly connect with you to seize an opportunity or just as quickly dismiss you and walk away. They may shake your hand and engage in a conversation while one eye is watching for the next potential client to walk through the door.

The challenge is to get their attention and gain their trust. The gift is to overlook the rough edges and understand where the survival instincts originate to bring compassion to the communication.

There's More?

Contributed by Victoria B.

I was sitting in a workshop getting ready to put together my speaker sheet when one of the other participants sat down at the table next to me.

She pulled out four binders, then plastic binder holders, a stapler, a tape dispenser, her computer with a fan for it to sit on, vitamins, a protein shake, and a manila folder filled with paper. As a Cheerleader Character Code, I was in a trance watching her pulling all these things from her bag.

Besides being totally distracted now, I looked down at the space where I was writing and it was gone.

This person had taken up not only the area in front of her, but also half of the area in front of me. My frustration quickly bubbled. Something inside me wanted to tell her to get off my side.

I then remembered, oh, she is an Actress Character Code. Recalling what I had learned, Actors do everything bigger.

Realizing that, I could speak to her with a fresh awareness. I politely asked her to move her things over a bit so that I could also have space to write, and she kindly responded.

Speaking

Like the Cheerleader Character Code, Actors are also talkers and blurters. They may interrupt, talk over you, or always be the first to respond, raising their hand or just shouting out the answer. Their attitude of "move in or miss out" shows not just in their body language, but also in their speaking style.

Actors are often the loudest in the room and seemingly less aware (or uninterested) in how people are responding to them. They can be very funny, although their humor can be sarcastic or biting at times.

An Actor may make a cutting remark directly to you, and it may take a few beats before you realize the impact of what he or she said. Actors are great storytellers, but they often command the spotlight and do not allow others to join in the conversation.

Their speaking style is direct, bold, and convincing. They can easily overpower other Character Codes who speak in a different style that is slower and less commanding.

Actors can be inflammatory or accusatory in their communication. The best way to interact with them to diffuse a situation is to allow them to have the lion's share of the emotion while you remain objective. They are natural fighters and can engage quickly.

An Actor is also likely to say the unexpected or ask you questions that may surprise you. It is never boring when you are conversing with an Actor, whose repertoire runs the gamut from raucous humor to cutting remarks to grandiose tales. Equally surprising can be the range of emotions and loyalty expressed—from complete dismissal to instant bosom buddies. It will be a wild ride.

Psyche

The four driving needs that influence the majority of our decisions include *certainty*, *variety*, *significance*, and *connection*. Understanding a Character Code's particular driving need is key to successfully connecting with them.

Driving Need

Actors are driven by an inner desire to *be* right. They crave praise, attention, leadership, validation, and authority. This feeds their driving need for significance and the spotlight that provides recognition for their talents.

Before you just write Actors off with a few choice adjectives, consider where their strong personality traits come from—they've survived many challenges throughout their life. Some experienced regular feedback that they weren't good enough, and others have come from a truly tough childhood. Their default of having to focus on self and get ahead is a carryover of what was needed to make it through early life. Unfortunately, if Actors continue in this way, they self-perpetuate the pattern.

Character Traits

Actors are fast paced, commanding, and always noticeable. They range from being a fun shopping buddy with whom you spend too much money to an overbearing, demanding, and insensitive personality who's tough to be around.

Actors are often capable of getting tasks done that other people don't want to do. That's why, when channeled correctly, Actors can move nations of people into action and make huge social changes. Some of the more memorable, dramatic, and revolutionary figures in history were Actors. Napoleon is a good example.

Actors exert a powerful influence; their presence is palpable. They seek the approval and praise of others, up to a point. If they are shunned or rejected, they will often use this as fuel to motivate themselves and be more determined in their course of action.

Although they seek social stimulation, they also have a wall around them blocking other people from getting close. Because of this, they may seem distant or superficial. Both male and female Actors struggle with being abrupt or insensitive and plowing over some of the other Character Codes who can't handle them. As a result, many Actors struggle to have true friends. Actresses often find it difficult to have friendships with other women. This is because an unbalanced Actress can be blunt and insensitive. Actresses usually get along better with men.

Actors are funny and often use humor as a tool to keep people entertained, but more important, they also use humor to keep people emotionally disconnected. This helps maintain that defensive wall of protection around them. Actors are direct about how they feel, in particular how they feel about you. They will inquire about your life in the most personal ways. In a state of awareness an Actor will take special care to be sensitive and allow other Character Codes to express themselves.

Actors can be fiercely protective. When you have an Actor as a real friend, he or she will take on any fight for you and be your champion. If you earn the respect of an Actor, he or she can be fiercely loyal. That said, it is tough to earn the respect of Actors because they are judgmental, critical, competitive, and very resistant to trust.

In an emotionally healthy state, the Actor can be very motivating and will support others in any way possible. When Actors decide to take on the mission of making everything right in the world, there's no limit to what they can accomplish. They have the energy, power, confidence, persuasion, and influence to make things happen.

The Inner Meanie

The Actors' inner meanie tells them they're not good enough, pretty enough, or talented enough, and sometimes not worthy of love. They may present strongly as confident and fearless; however, it is an attempt to cover up this negative voice that says they are inherently flawed.

Business Derailed by Breakfast

I had the opportunity to observe how quickly an Actor can take over a boardroom and declare mutiny with a group of business professionals.

At these all-day meetings, breakfast, lunch, and dinner were provided with the understanding that each meal would be prepped by a personal chef.

It turned out that breakfast was supplied by the business assistant. As it still included a fine selection and I was there to perform work, I wasn't concerned.

The Actor, on the other hand, was starting to rile up the group.

He began by whispering that this was a bait-and-switch tactic and then went into full-blown speech mode regarding ethics and the need for a refund. By the time he was done, the entire room was whipped into a fury over the $15 breakfast.

Of course, the inner meanie never speaks the truth, but it can be hard to silence that critical voice in your head. We all respond differently to this type of self-sabotage. Actors typically counter by trying to outrun it to prove it wrong, seeking ways to shine and demonstrate their star power.

The best way to overcome our inner meanie is to face it. Nonetheless, many Actors do not want to explore or dive deep into the wounds that created this feeling of being internally broken. Much of the Actor's strong persona is a survival mechanism to cover significant emotional pain.

When an Actor is willing to move from trying to outrun his or her inner meanie to looking within, the shift is tangible.

Access the resource "Taming the Actor Meanie" for tips and insight (and a little humor) at http://charactercode.com/actormeanie.

Conflict, Stress, and Emotions

Actors often don't have a good outlet for the fire they feel inside. Without a resource to pour that energy into, they will pick on petty stuff or tear down the greatness in others. Actors can quickly rally supporters when they are unhappy, being capable of inflaming a crowd or starting a riot in an airport after a long delay.

Actors in an unhealthy state can be draining, exhausting, argumentative, difficult, and dramatic and can be an overall challenge to work with. In an unbalanced situation, they will love to argue, evaluate circumstances with a "me-versus-them" mentality, and feel they are the ultimate authority. Often, this is a cover-up for their lack of security and self-esteem.

In contrast, Actors in a healthy, aware state will be sensitive of others and are often the life of the party. Everyone will want to be around them because of their expressive humor and their ease with communication. In this balanced situation, they will be jovial, motivate others, and be a lot of fun—the ideal travel buddy.

Health and Wellness

The Actor is the Character Code most likely to be a hypochondriac. Actors often know of every disease and may be convinced they are dying of something. They may use health issues or crises as a way to fuel their need for significance. They also run the risk of having a real condition overlooked because of their false alarms and hyperbole in the past.

Actors typically stick with Western medical practice and only dabble in alternative therapies once they feel traditional medicine has failed them. Although initially very skeptical, if they are won over, they will rave about their new practitioner or the alternative practice as if they personally discovered it.

But Actors can be very fickle. If they become dissatisfied with their practitioner, they will be just as vocal about how someone is a quack.

Jobs and Careers

Actors are capable of succeeding in any demanding profession. However, they thrive and shine when their performance or success is based on their own effort. They prefer being in the limelight to working in a team or participating in collaborative activities.

Many people who work in entertainment are Actors, largely in response to the range of emotions, high energy, and public exposure in that industry. It feeds their need for significance, and its spotlight requires a special Character Code to withstand the pressure. Many Actors are successful but may struggle with personal relationships and inner satisfaction.

Actors prefer a work situation that tracks results, provides incentives, and rewards meeting goals or quotas. They like a system that allows them latitude to be who they are and bend the rules.

Marketing and Sales

Probably an Actor's greatest fear is that he or she has no real purpose or point in life. Actors need a cause to live and fight for. Their nightmare usually involves living a life that doesn't matter.

In contrast, the Actors' dream may involve living a purposeful life of influence and being recognized for their amazing talents. They are typically unaware that this is the why behind that gnawing feeling of unease when they don't have a way to focus the fire in their belly. They feel most satisfied when they have something to champion.

When marketing to Actors, paint a picture that allows them to star as the hero. Compelling design for an Actor can range from classic to romantic, as long as the overall look is polished. Actors like the look of money. Make sure your message conveys competence, success, accomplishment, and savvy.

Study this section so you understand the problems that Actors need to resolve. They are a tough crowd because they are often unaware of or uninterested in obvious problems that need to be solved, such as their people skills. Some suggestions for solutions could be learning sophisticated time management (they have the basics down), connecting with clients, training staff, maintaining their health, handling conflict, or increasing their public persona and star status. Appeal to their ambition.

Actress Out of Hiding

I consulted with an Actress who had been unsuccessful in filling her business presentations with her ideal clients. She had been branded several times by advisors who were attempting to fit her into a traditional box.

Instead, I created a brand that emphasized everything about her that was an Actress, the pizzazz, the excitement, the self-promotion, and the desire to be a business celebrity.

As a result, her next training was filled with her ideal clients, she got to be herself, and best of all, her sales tripled!

The Ideal Client

If Actors are your ideal clients, it is essential to make a first impression that shows you can handle them. If they feel they can push you around, you will never have their respect. You will need to be firm, strong, determined, and specific and have clear boundaries within your business. Actors will test those boundaries and try to rewrite your rules.

As I mentioned in a previous section, Actors are also talkers and like to share stories. They will definitely exaggerate; listening to them talk can be like live theater. Don't schedule back-to-back appointments with two Actors, because you will never arrive at the second on time.

Actors are the only Character Code that prefers the company of others more than their own like-minded counterparts. Actors do not want to be around other Actors. They don't like sharing the spotlight. Two Actors can really clash.

Actors prefer a more acquiescing Cheerleader or maybe an Activist, although they probably feel the Activist is too "woo-woo." Most Activists are scared of Actors. Artists are the most compatible with Actors; they share the same driving need for significance. But since the Artist doesn't crave the spotlight, the Actor feels understood and able to shine without having to compete for attention. More on how the Character Codes connect with one another in Chapter 9.

When it comes to deciding to become your client or buy from you, Actors can be the most challenging of the Character Codes. They may reach a decision quickly and then become easily overwhelmed and fail to follow through. Sometimes it can be tough to grab their attention in the first place and earn their respect. If Actors are your ideal clients, this is important to know. You need to structure your business model to allow for their behavioral style.

I believe the Actor is one of the Character Codes most in need of some nurturing, but Actors often don't get it because people have a hard time getting close to them. You are providing a service in this world if you can nurture an out-of-balance Actor. Assist in bringing an Actor into balance, and that person will be a star pupil or client success story.

Summarizing the Actor

If you are an Actor, or it's at least one of your top two Character Codes, you can start by being more nurturing and loving toward yourself. When you notice that inner meanie speaking negatively about how you are broken, aren't good enough, or don't matter, remind yourself that this meanie is just part of being an Actor and can take the night off. Remember what you have survived and accomplished just to be here today.

Advice for the Actor

Life will be more enjoyable if you don't always focus on being right or trying to prove your value. Accept that you have inherent value and focus on making *others* right.

When you are the Actor and are feeling like everyone around you is an idiot, remind yourself that this is just a feeling. There's no way everyone else is always wrong. There are many ways to get something done, and yours is only one of them.

As an Actor, when you understand and make allowances for the other Character Codes, you have the power to be a positive voice for change and are a force to be reckoned with.

Advice for Interacting with Actors

If you aren't an Actor but your ideal client is, you need to have thick skin and occasionally be ready for combat. Don't take anything the Actor says personally. When you consider the visual and verbal message you must send to communicate effectively, be sure your message screams confidence and power. Actors will not respect you or take you seriously if you cannot address them as an equal.

Review the "Appearance," "Presentation," and "Speaking" sections of the Actor. See what little things you can add to make your ideal client comfortable. This isn't about getting dressed in costume, but about honoring who you are and making sure your message lands with your audience. Actors aren't looking for you to look like them! They would then see you as competition. Rather, they want to know that you are competent and up to the challenge.

Make sure you know that the Actor is the right client for you. Your other option would be to pick a different client who is more connected to you or more compatible with your business.

First Impressions with the Actor

When meeting an Actor for the first time, be sure you look pulled together and savvy in your every move and everything you say. An Actor will still initially doubt your ability and your credibility, so be on your toes. Actors are sharp, quick, and witty; you'll need to be able to match them to win their business. Move in quickly with a firm hand-shake, look into their eyes, and be unwavering. If you appear hesitant or vague or seem to lack confidence, it will be a turnoff. The best personality for working with Actors is someone who can match their power, intelligence, and speed but is very unemotional and doesn't flinch at anything the Actor throws at him or her.

Here are some things you can do to enhance your first impression that elicits *respect* from an Actor:

>> Avoid being very dramatic in style even though the Actor may be.
>> Dress conservatively and demonstrate fashion sense.
>> Achieve an overall look that is tailored, with attention to details.
>> Dress nicely, but not too businesslike.
>> Make eye contact.

Here are some aspects that send a warning or spell out danger to an Actor and should be avoided:

>> You look sloppy or messy.
>> You show up unprepared.
>> You seem too woo-woo or overly sensitive.
>> You are another Actor.

Actors as your ideal Character Code client can range from less flamboyant in personality and style to over the top. So consider with what level of Actor you feel most comfortable working with and how to best serve the Actor in your business. One of the greatest strengths that Actors have is their ability to move mountains when their energy is effectively channeled.

How to Read a Client Now

Now that you have read the Actor Character Code in detail, you'll want to remember to:

» Begin your "people watching" with new eyes and see how many Actors you can find—they are often the easiest to spot!

» Notice how the driving need for significance dictates the Actor's behavior and appearance and start identifying the patterns you see.

» Consider if the Actor is the right ideal Character Code client for you.

» Observe what, if any, changes you would need to make in your personal branding to make sure you can communicate with the Actor.

» Begin to feel more compassion for Actors (or yourself) when you consider their inner meanie and what you learned in the "Psyche" section.

In Chapter 6 you will learn how to identify a Scholar Character Code. This will include all the details you need to better communicate with, connect to, attract, and read Scholars from across the room.

Take the following action steps now:

» Download the "Actor Character Code Overview" to have the details and color sketches right at your fingertips at http://charactercode.com/actor.

» Access the resource "Taming the Actor Meanie" for tips and insight (and a little humor) at http://charactercode.com/actormeanie.

SIX

The Scholar Character Code

Where's the Evidence?

NAMED THIS CHARACTER Code the Scholar to provoke the image of a person who is studious, methodical, and analytical. Scholars are great thinkers and researchers and are often experts in their fields.

Scholars have a driving need for certainty, and they are very task oriented. Of all the Character Codes, Scholars can sometimes be the most difficult to pick out of a crowd. Why? Their mindset is function over fashion, and they do not identify with their appearance. Instead, they will make their appearance choices based on what they consider a requisite appropriate to the setting and environment.

Take, for example, the common picture of a group of male lawyers wearing the expected corporate suit. The men in tailored black suits are the Class President Character Code, but the guy wearing a slightly older suit—no pizzazz, perhaps the jacket and trousers are not matching, but nonetheless neat—is the Scholar. Does he look a little disheveled? Then he's an Activist-Scholar combo. Scholars wear a suit because that's what lawyers are *supposed* to wear, but they do not particularly care nor identify with the suit itself.

This is also true of Scholar women. They will appear tidy and neat, and you might mistake them at first for another Character Code. But something will be off about their look. A Scholar woman might wear last year's dress style, or a Scholar man will carry an old briefcase because it is the function and not the form that matters for Scholars. Even when they appear indifferent to their appearance, Scholars still communicate to us how they want to be regarded by others. Here is how to read them from across the room.

Appearance

Those things we care most about are reflected in our appearance, and so we are constantly giving clues to others about how we want to be treated.

Hair

Depending on the level of rigidity in the Scholar, the Scholar's hair will range from having every strand in place to looking past due for a cut. For a Scholar woman, this may mean a neat ponytail with no bumps or loose strands; it's neatly pulled back and gathered. Or if she's more fashion aware, she may select a precision bob. Some Scholar women will wear a very short hairstyle.

A Scholar woman is unlikely to use any hair embellishments or color or apply anything that would attract attention. She will also want a style that is very easy to maintain—ideally "wash and go."

Scholar men most commonly wear a short, conservative cut and are typically clean shaven. Some Scholar men will wear less fashionable styles such as a comb-over or a middle part.

Makeup

The Scholar woman wears simple makeup, if any at all. This Character Code is not interested in the latest fashion trends and will do only enough to appear as she deems proper for her environment. This often means wearing as little makeup as her career requires—ideally none at all. She may even be indifferent to how she looks. Functionality always trumps fashion for Scholars.

Jewelry

The Scholar Character Code woman doesn't typically wear jewelry. If there is a purpose to the jewelry that makes sense to the Scholar (such as looking more professional), then she will wear it.

The jewelry has a purpose, and it fits into a system of attire. The jewelry, as with her makeup choice, will reflect what she has to do to appear appropriate and acceptable in her environment. Her style would most likely include sleek lines, simple metals, and a small or petite form. Typical earrings (if any) would be simple studs.

Scholar men won't wear additional jewelry outside a simple wedding band and a functional wristwatch.

Clothing

As with hair and makeup choices, the Scholar will wear clothing appropriate for work. Unlike many other Character Codes, Scholars are not driven by a desire to be fashionable or noticeable, and they aren't really invested in what they wear. That disconnect is what has them showing up in a look that seems "off"—sometimes precision neat, sometimes rumpled, old-fashioned, or inconsistent, because they don't personally identify with their appearance.

Typical Scholar clothing choices would be simple slacks or a dress, likely very plain, without much detail, and the focus definitely on function. If a Scholar is required to wear a suit, it's likely to be black, blue, gray, or another dark, solid color. If you see a Scholar dressed like a Cheerleader or some other atypical look, it is because the Scholar is in a setting where he or she thinks such attire is required. Overall, Scholar men and women will appear less fashionable than those around them.

I base most of my fashion sense on what doesn't itch.

—Gilda Radner, comedienne

Accessories

The Scholar woman, unlike the Cheerleader, is the Character Code most likely to use the same purse for all occasions. It is plain and functional and in a dark, solid color. The size is typically small, containing little more than a wallet and perhaps a single tube of lip gloss. It usually has a large handle or a long strap so it can be worn over her shoulder. She does not carry a purse with a short handle, and it's very unlikely that she owns a clutch at all, since both would be impractical. The Scholar's purse often shows signs of wear, such as edges slightly frayed, because she's had it for a long time.

Scholar men often have briefcases that are functional and not very stylish. As with the Scholar's purse, the Scholar's briefcase is also likely to show signs of wear, all pointing to the Scholar's preference for function over fashion. The Scholar may use the same briefcase for decades.

Nails

Scholar Character Codes avoid using nail polish altogether, or if they do, it's typically clear. Their nails are clean and kept closely cut. The Scholar is the least likely to have painted toenails. Most Scholars would feel that getting a manicure or pedicure was an inefficient use of time or feel like a fish out of water in such a situation.

Shoes

Footwear is another great insight into personality. There's a huge variation in footwear within each Character Code regarding style, color, sturdiness, and the care we take of them. Shoes speak to who we are and what we care about. If you see either a man or a woman wearing loafers, chances are that person is a Scholar. Scholars love practical, comfortable, sturdy, and fully functional shoes. For women, if she must wear heels, it's almost always a black pump with a half-inch or one-inch heel.

Scholars will always pick a shoe that serves the purpose of getting them from point A to point B before they consider (if ever) choosing shoes for style or fashion or for the sake of coordinating with an outfit. For this reason, Scholars typically own the fewest pairs of shoes of any of the Character Codes.

Presentation

The Scholar loves to project a knowledgeable presence. Notice I wrote presence because a Scholar would be turned off by the word *energy*. Scholars strive to be the experts in their field. Therefore, they will be the most rigid of all the Character Codes in their posture, holding themselves straight up and down. Scholars live up in their heads and not in their bodies.

Scholars do not normally make eye contact. They are thinkers. When Scholars weigh evidence or are thinking or remembering something, they often look away as they recall the information. They are not being snooty or rude; being in perpetual contemplation, they are just doing what they do best.

The Scholar is no fan of physical contact and most definitely not a hugger. If you run up to a Scholar and hug him or her, you're likely to feel the person's body stiffen like a board. Don't be offended if you don't get a hug back. However, Scholars will shake hands, but it will be a brief handshake, perhaps only one up and one downward motion.

If you see a Scholar across the room, he or she may be standing off to one side holding up a wall instead of mixing with others in the middle of the room. Scholars aren't "people persons." They prefer data, research, and their own thoughts. However, they will interact when work requires it. Perhaps the most useful way to think of Scholars is that they prefer solitude to crowds. They don't mind being in their office, by themselves, getting their job done.

When speaking to Scholars, give them physical space. Of all the Character Codes, they are the most likely to need a lot of personal space. (The Activist stands the closest.) In fact, Scholars move their bodies the least of all the Character Codes. They can appear snooty to others, but really it's just their Character Code reflecting their desire to follow the rules and to be accurate, effective, and correct.

Speaking

The Scholar Character Code is a researcher. Scholars are not verbose, and when you ask them questions you may receive very short answers. They like to process details and data and learn the system underlying any type of knowledge. For example, of all the Character Codes, the Scholar is the one who wants to know, in minute detail, your process.

Scholars are generally not communicative unless you are talking about a topic they have researched and know a lot about. If the topic is of interest to them, they may go on in painstaking detail about it. Most times, however, they will be quiet and only say what must be said, because they are not fans of small talk, nor are they very good at it. Their speech patterns also reveal a more functionally based mindset.

In addition to finding chitchat difficult, Scholars aren't always tuned in to the reactions of others. For example, many Scholars won't notice if others are really listening or interested in hearing all the details they are sharing. Scholars also talk in an even tone without a great deal of animation. They often are precise in their language and maintain high standards in their manner of speaking.

The Scholar is usually well educated and prefers to speak in terms of facts instead of emotions. Scholars avoid colorful language and are the least likely to exaggerate.

Scholars tend toward honesty, but some may be too brutal in their delivery because of a desire to be factual regardless of others' feelings. They aren't sentimental and will use the least amount of words necessary to communicate—unless you touch on a topic they find intellectually stimulating.

Psyche

If we are to understand ourselves and others, we must first understand how driving needs impact our lives. The four driving needs that influence the majority of our decisions are *certainty, variety, significance,* and *connection.*

Driving Need

The Scholar is driven by an inner desire for certainty. If you think of a computer chip speaking its binary language of on and off, then you can better understand the Scholar. Most Scholars are unsettled by shades of gray or even the word maybe. They prefer a definitive system of yes and no, right and wrong, black and white.

Some Scholars will be diligent in their pursuit of solving the great problems in science or other subjects, in an attempt to bring certainty to unknown mysteries.

Their driving need will prevent most Scholars from making impulsive decisions or being spontaneous. In some cases this is prudent, and in other situations it can lead to a fairly tame existence. They are likely to have a routine and stick to it.

Character Traits

Scholars are logical and pragmatic. They are great at troubleshooting and have high executive reasoning skills. They are task oriented, methodical, and systematic, and they appreciate fact gathering and data collection. They place more weight on objective evidence than do other Character Codes and are not typically interested in opinions or intuition. This is why they prefer work to social situations. When they are working alone, they can perform the analytical skills that are their strength.

Scholars tend to be serious people. The can appear formal or reserved. While Cheerleaders bounce from person to person or group to group in a social setting, Scholars move methodically, taking their time to decide with whom to speak and, once conversing, what to say.

Scholars can be a phenomenal source of knowledge and data. They can be the go-to person to create systems for whatever process is needed. But Scholars who are not well balanced can become obsessed with perfection. This may keep them from completing a task because, well, it is never done quite right. They can also suffer from tunnel vision, seeing only one idea or one task and avoiding the larger picture that may include other peoples' feelings. They can also use questions and data collecting as a means to create distance between themselves and others.

For Scholars, any work or learning experience is better if they are able to just depend on themselves to get the job done. If they are not hung up on perfection, Scholars are wonderful at completing tasks. They don't appreciate group projects and balk at the networking and referral process. To them, networking may seem like a fruitless interaction without any guaranteed outcome, versus just getting their work done.

I Have an Emergency!

The preference for certainty has most Scholars working overtime to avoid unpredictable situations. Sometimes even the slightest disturbance in their routine can cause them to become overwhelmed, leaving behind their normally rational mindset, and behave as if in crisis.

One such example was a previous Scholar assistant that came running in one morning and said she didn't think she could work that day because an emergency came up.

I thought a family member was ill or there was a fire or some other dramatic situation. So I asked her what was wrong.

Her reply, "The window on my car won't roll up."

Sometimes Scholars rely too heavily on technology and use it as a barrier to connecting with people in real life. Or they may use technology as their favorite source of human connection and communication. Scholars may sometimes prefer a night at home with their thoughts to dining with friends.

The Inner Meanie

The Scholars' inner meanie tells them they are not smart enough or they didn't do it right. Depending on their ability to deal with this, some may avoid doing anything in their lives at which they don't think they can excel.

Many Scholars beat themselves up for not being spontaneous or for not being like the other faster-paced Character Codes around them. It is much better for Scholars to realize their way of looking at the world is a gift in many professions. You wouldn't want a top researcher to become bored with his or her work before coming to a solution. Nor would you want an author to give up on writing a book because it wouldn't write itself fast enough. Scholars, just as all the other Character Codes, have their inherent value and strengths.

The driving need for certainty and an inner meanie that questions whether they are smart or right are the reasons why Scholars can become very vested in being right and arguing their point of view as fact.

Access the resource "Taming the Scholar Meanie" for tips and insight (and a little humor) at http://charactercode.com/scholarmeanie.

Conflict, Stress, and Emotions

Of all the Character Codes, Scholars struggle the most with expressing emotions and feelings and relating to others. They may find human relationships challenging. Of course, there is a wide variation in the way they respond, ranging from one who gets along fine with others but dislikes parties and small talk to another who has no social skills and truly prefers avoiding all interactions with another person.

Scholars can be difficult to read because they aren't very animated in their facial expressions or their body language. Scholars don't like conflict and may sometimes give in to avoid it, but you will quickly become aware if they are displeased or do not agree with you.

Scholars who are not well balanced can hold grudges and may even plan revenge. Scholars can benefit from learning people skills to better relate to others around them. They could also benefit from exploring feelings, emotions, and the gray areas in life.

Identifying Scholars

Scholars struggle the most with understanding that they are a Scholar Character Code even when it is obvious to everyone else. Part of this is because they overthink it and make it more difficult than it needs to be. Another reason is because they really don't care about nor do they identify with their appearance choices the same way other Character Codes do.

What this means is that Scholars will often wear the same thing all the time, or they may wear a variety of clothing options that don't seem the least bit related.

When I first started working with a new assistant, she asked which Character Code she was. Scholar, I replied. She asked, "How can that be, when I have on a Cheerleader shirt, Activist shoes, and an Artist necklace, and I have a Class President haircut?" I told her she just answered the question.

Some days she would show up for work dressed like a runner, some days in a dress with nylons, some days like a college student—always different and never a cohesive look.

It took her a little while to realize she was a Scholar. She had to read everything and analyze her life before she agreed with my conclusion about her that I had made from first meeting her.

One of the things that made her laugh as a Scholar was remembering a past experience with a relationship that didn't end on good terms. The ex-boyfriend had left her stuck with some video rental charges.

She orchestrated a plan to call his workplace and pretend to be the video store, asking the nice office receptionist when the ex-boyfriend planned on returning his adult videos, naming some outrageous, imaginary titles.

"Oh, my," said my assistant, "I not only planned the revenge but also carried it through."

She was earning her third master's degree and rewriting her thesis . . . but it still took her a long time to come to terms with being the Scholar Character Code!

Health and Wellness

Healthwise, the Scholar tends to be uninterested in alternative health and is likely to place all reliance on Western medicine and the latest double-blind study. If Scholars are attracted to alternative health, then they will want to know the research and data that back it up.

Scholars prefer a regimen with rules. They are good about following a program exactly how it is laid out once they think it is effective. Some lean toward extreme behavior regarding their health and can be very rigid in their practices if they believe in the benefits. If they have come to a conclusion about what are the "proper" actions to maintain a healthy lifestyle, they may be very judgmental about those that don't take their advice and follow the same plan.

Jobs and Careers

Many Scholars choose analytical professions such as professors, processors, engineers, researchers, accountants, and scientists, largely in response to the organized, detailed, and finite qualities those jobs possess.

Scholars can be good at accomplishing goals, but they may take longer than needed, and that can irritate other Character Codes who are faster paced and prefer that deadlines be met—if not surpassed.

In a healthy state, the Scholar can provide the backbone for the systems that keep a business or organization running smoothly. You won't have to worry about whether every *t* will be crossed when you have a Scholar in charge. In other words, you can rest easy knowing that every task will be done accurately and meticulously, particularly when Scholars have their name tied to it and have control over the outcome.

Some Scholars are inventive, using their vast bank of knowledge to reinvent a better system than the one currently in use. They do prefer working on one problem at a time and will become vested in their own solution. In contrast, most Class Presidents would quickly move from one potential solution to another, not caring so much about who completed it or how, as long as it was done.

Scholars can run into trouble with group dynamics if others challenge their opinion. Scholars tend to believe they are right because they have examined all the facts and have come to the only logical conclusion. A great example of this is the character Spock from the television program *Star Trek*.

Marketing and Sales

A Scholar's greatest fear is being thrown into an environment where people display their humanity in an unorganized, unprofessional, or offensive manner. This could be a jail cell, Miami during spring break, Mardi Gras, or a family reunion. Any environment that has a lot of people—that is unpredictable and lacks order—would be challenging for the Scholar.

Scholars' dreams involve the completion of a project or invention of a system they created followed by recognition of their efforts. However, Scholars' nightmares involve feeling criticized, challenged, rushed, and unappreciated for their knowledge. If you are addressing a crowd of Scholars, you will want to acknowledge their intellect, reasoning, and analytical skills. Stay factual and avoid language laden with feelings and emotions.

Scholar in Charge

I knew a man who ran a corporate department that was in charge of numerous social and PR activities for the business; he handled publicity and meet and greets, and he planned multiple functions and gatherings each year. Whenever new people came in or out of the corporation, they invariably met this man. As a Cheerleader Character Code, he excelled in the people department.

With all those business events and people, this department also generated a great deal of paperwork, tracking, and follow-up to manage.

That was not this Cheerleader's strength.

His office looked like a strong gust of wind had blown papers everywhere. Left to his own devices, he would make promises to clients that were forgotten, schedule meetings with colleagues that were missed, and be overbudget and behind schedule with his event planning.

What was his saving grace? His Scholar assistant.

While he was the face of the department and the king in people management, she created the order, the systems, the tracking, and the follow-through that kept the department running.

Clients and colleagues learned that when they needed something from him, to make sure the request went through his Scholar assistant so it would get done!

When marketing to a Scholar, keep things simple and tightly focused on cause-and-effect relationships. Use measured tones and speak clearly and confidently. Make sure your message conveys trust and competence and drives home the point that you have a system or method based on verifiable data or results.

When asked to make a decision, Scholars weigh the information carefully before deciding what to do. Selling to Scholars can be a very slow sales cycle because they need to think through their decision and weigh every detail of your offer before they will commit.

Where you can provide a useful solution is in helping Scholars deal with managing people, connecting with clients, outsourcing projects, and addressing their difficulty with the imperfect aspects that life brings their way.

The Ideal Client

If the Scholar is your ideal client, you must offer a first impression that shows that you are competent, pulled together, and organized and that demonstrates that you appreciate solutions from provable data. You will then need to have patience regardless of whether you make sales from the stage, online, from a presentation, or in one-on-one meetings with clients. It would be wise to have systems built into your business that provide reliable data and quantifiable information about your product. Present your solution as a system or process.

Scholars prefer to be around other Scholars like themselves. Scholars may also like being with the Class President due to the Class President's directness and focus on tasks. Scholars are the least compatible with Cheerleaders and Actors, although the Scholars may find them socially intriguing.

Summarizing the Scholar

If you are the Scholar, or it's at least one of your top two Character Codes, you can start by being kinder to yourself and acknowledging that nothing is ever perfect. When you notice that inner meanie speaking negatively about how you aren't smart enough or telling you that you didn't do something right, ask, "Who's to say what is right?" And of course you are smart, and you don't need to prove it. We all know it.

Advice for the Scholar

When you are feeling irritated or angry with those around you, remind yourself this is just a feeling. We are all competent in some ways and incompetent in others. Clearly, the world is full of people who may view the world differently than you do. Not everything is black and white, right and wrong. That's only in your thinking.

Acknowledge that gray areas do exist, and without the gray, the world would be a much less interesting place. Shake things up now and then and vary your routine; see what happens when you stretch your comfort zone.

Advice for Interacting with Scholars

If you aren't a Scholar but your ideal client is, you need to consider the visual and verbal messages necessary to communicate effectively. A Scholar desires to be factual and detailed and is uninterested in drama or other emotions. Don't run up to a Scholar and give him or her a big hug.

Instead, look professional and behave according to society's standards based upon the particular situation in which you find yourself. Scholars appreciate good manners, a keen mind, and proper behavior. They tend to be more reserved. You will lose credibility with long-winded and overly personal stories.

Review the "Appearance, "Presentation," and "Speaking" sections and consider how best to connect with the Scholar crowd. This isn't about trying to act more intellectual than you really are, but it won't hurt to put in the extra work if you want to serve Scholar clients. Scholars really do want to know your process forward and backward so they can feel certain about their purchase.

If you work in an industry or offer a service that is tough to quantify, you may want to select a different ideal client.

First Impressions with the Scholar

When meeting a Scholar for the first time, present yourself in a formal, businesslike manner. Don't act overly familiar. Don't move or talk too fast and don't stand too close. Scholars appreciate personal space. Speak factually and explain the details freely. Remember that Scholars want to know the steps, not just the results. Play to their process-oriented minds, their desire for due diligence.

Here are some things you can do to add to your look that will enhance your *credibility* with a Scholar:

> » Wear jewelry that is simple and professional with clean lines.
> » Look pulled together and professional.
> » Dress in solid, conservative colors.
> » Wear a suit or tailored clothing.
> » Choose a hairstyle that is more contained.

Here are some elements of a first impression that a Scholar disdains:

> » You look flamboyant or display drama.
> » You wear loud, garish clothing.
> » You move really fast or laugh really loud.
> » You are constantly vague, not covering any real content.

If the Scholar is your ideal client, be careful about stressing any kind of urgency or rush to a decision unless it is backed by a legitimate need. Be very clear with expectations and deadlines, e.g., project management timetables, materials deliverables, and dates by which preparatory tasks need to be completed.

One of the Scholar's greatest strengths is being able to create the process and then execute the steps needed to see a project to its conclusion. That's why Scholars are often the backbone of a business or institution. When they complete a task, job, or process, you can be assured it has been accomplished thoroughly and accurately and to spec. They desire to do a job well.

How to Read a Client Now

Now that you have read the Scholar Character Code in detail, you'll want to remember to:

» Begin your "people watching" with new eyes and see how many Scholars you can find.

» Notice how the driving need for certainty dictates the Scholar's behavior and appearance and start identifying the patterns you see.

» Consider if the Scholar is the right ideal Character Code client for you.

» Observe what, if any, changes you would need to make in your personal branding to make sure you can communicate with the Scholar.

» Begin to feel more compassion for Scholars (or yourself) when you consider their inner meanie and what you learned in the "Psyche" section.

In Chapter 7 you will learn how to identify an Activist Character Code. This will include all the details you need to better communicate with, connect to, attract, and read Activists from across the room.

Take the following action steps now:

» Download the "Scholar Character Code Overview" to have the details and color sketches right at your fingertips at http://charactercode.com/scholar.

» Access the resource "Taming the Scholar Meanie" for tips and insight (and a little humor) at http://charactercode.com/scholarmeanie.

SEVEN

The Activist Character Code

Let's All Get Along

THE NEXT CHARACTER Code is called the Activist because I wanted you to get a picture in your head of someone that is ready to take up a cause and cares a great deal about people, animals, or feelings. An Activist's driving need is for connection, and an Activist cares more about someone's humanity than any other factor.

Activists are very easy to identify in a crowded room based on their appearance and their behavior even before you hear them speak. Activists tend to move at a slower pace and take their time making decisions. They greatly benefit from being a part of a community that supports and nurtures them. They will often make buying decisions based on a group consensus.

By now, you are aware of the way I describe each Character Code: appearance, presentation, and speaking style, breaking each down into descriptive terms that apply to the individual Character Codes. Are you an Activist? Can you think of some Activists you know? Let's take a closer look at how to read them from across the room.

Appearance

The things we care most about are reflected in our appearance, and we are constantly giving clues to others about how we want to be treated.

Hair

The Activist's hair is typically long for women. It can be wavy or straight and is often parted down the middle. Activists typically avoid using hair products, and so the Activist's hair is often the least styled of all the Character Codes. Activists have a more natural look. Women Activists typically do not dye their hair, and as Activists age, they are likely to show the natural gray or white instead of covering it up.

Activist men may have short hair that is fuller or grown out, looking in need of a cut. It may even be uncombed or unkempt looking. Some Activist men will wear longer hair or a braid. Many will wear facial hair with varying lengths of beard.

Makeup

An Activist's makeup is typically modest or natural, using muted tones and never in excess. This is the Character Code most likely to forgo any makeup at all, even if it seems required for work or a social situation. Activists are more likely to use lip balm or creams while avoiding makeup. They also prefer natural, chemical-free products that they feel are healthier for their body and the environment.

Jewelry

Activist women typically wear less jewelry than many of the other Character Codes, aside from the Scholar. Activists may wear beads or medallions and favor stones, shells, quartz, turquoise, or semiprecious or genuine stones. The choice of jewelry reflects their earthiness and may include natural cords, even twine or hemp.

The jewelry that both Activist women and men wear often has sentimental value. Many Activists who wear jewelry feel it empowers them, protects them, inspires them, or serves as a talisman of some kind. I have teased my Activist friends that their favorite necklace is the rock their spouse found on the beach, cleaned up, wrapped with twine, and gave to them in a paper bag. Activists don't relish pomp and circumstance; it is the meaning behind the item that counts the most. They often wear the same jewelry all the time.

Activists are the Character Code most likely to wear a thumb ring or a toe ring, and they often exhibit very small body tattoos.

If Activist men wear jewelry, it is most likely a hemp necklace and a bracelet made of string or other natural fibers—which can be worn in a shower and do not need to be removed.

Clothing

Activists favor natural fibers and earthy colors. They don't all look like flower children; it is just an obvious and common identifier. The overall Activist look ranges from hippie flair to bohemian chic to Banana Republic basics to jeans with a T-shirt and vest. Activists lean toward more casual clothing, often worn in layers. Comfort is key, and it isn't surprising to see them in yoga gear all day long.

Activists are the Character Code least likely to wear black—and definitely not neon. Some Activists dress in outdoor gear and look like they are ready for a hike. A key component of their wardrobe might be a fleece vest. Women may wear long skirts. Depending on their work, they may be casual or dressy.

Accessories

An Activist's purse or bag is typically made of natural fibers, just like his or her clothes, with a long strap and worn over the head and across the opposite shoulder. To the Activist, comfort is the key to fashion, and a purse's function trumps its style.

Commonly an Activist woman will carry a knit purse or have multiple bags in which to carry her many items—she often has food packed when she is on the go. She may also be using the type of bags you bring to carry your own items from the grocery store.

Activist men often carry a backpack, the most likely of all adult Character Codes to do so. Activists are frequently seen carrying a Nalgene or glass water bottle and a bag of raw almonds for a snack. Some may carry a cooler for their food.

Nails

Activists typically wear no nail polish, nor do they keep their nails long. If they do anything to their nails at all, they may apply a clear polish for a more natural look. They often want to avoid the chemicals or formaldehyde in nail polish. More importantly, neither the upkeep nor the fashion statement behind painted nails holds much interest for them.

Shoes

Activists prefer to wear sandals and are the Character Code most likely to wear Birkenstocks. In a dressy mode, comfort would be a priority when picking a shoe instead of its looks. Most Activist women do not like wearing heels and will prefer flats.

The male Activist may also wear sandals or choose a tennis shoe or hiking boot. Regardless of the style, the shoes an Activist wears are likely to be worn and well used. Activists often buy the same style shoe over and over again or have only a few pairs they rotate.

An Activist Encounter

I was in a very Class President mindset when I was networking at a business function many years ago. I was focused on why I was there, how much time I had, what I needed to do, and how I would get out. This strategic thinking reflected in my short, direct, and businesslike manner at the event.

What I didn't expect was to run into an Activist during one of my purposeful walks in the room. When I met her, she put her hands on my shoulders and kept looking into my eyes. She didn't look away. I felt like she was searching for something. I started to feel uncomfortable and self-conscious.

She was kind, however, and allowed considerable space for me to talk. I felt like I had to say something. The next thing I knew, I was talking about losing a beloved pet years earlier. Tears welled up in my eyes. We connected and hugged.

Later I wondered, "What in the world just happened?" That was the last thing I had planned on talking about. Why had I shared such a personal story when I was there for work?

Now I laugh when I see similar interactions between an openhearted Activist and an unsuspecting Class President!

Presentation

Activists love to project a calming energy; their body stance is typically the most fluid of all the Character Codes. They're the most likely to sit cross-legged. They are more tuned in to their body and their heart versus living in their head.

Activists are huggers who hold those hugs, shake with both hands, or put their hands on your shoulders. If you see them from across the room, they may be engaged in a deep conversation with someone that appears intimate and concentrated, as if no one else is in the room.

When Activists feel stressed or overwhelmed, they may excuse themselves, physically leave the room, or retreat into sudden silence to reconnect with their source of strength. They typically lean forward in conversations and may stand very close to the person with whom they speak.

Activists are often very deliberate in their actions and movements, are thoughtful and mindful, and move with a more leisurely stride than the faster-paced Character Codes. Activists can give you the impression that they have all the time in the world. Rarely are they in a rush.

Activists will make eye contact with others and hold eye contact once it is established. This can be very positive for some people but unnerving for others, because Activists may give you the feeling they are looking right into the depths of your soul.

Speaking

The Activist is a listener. Activists are very good at letting you fully express yourself and waiting their turn before responding. They may even pause to take in what you've said before answering, or they might close their eyes for a moment to get their thoughts in order before replying.

Because of their calming nature, Activists are very good at drawing information out of people, sometimes simply by allowing them the time to communicate. I have seen other Character Codes become very unnerved when meeting an Activist once they discovered how good the Activist was at learning more about them—perhaps more than they wanted to share.

Activists are likely to talk in a steady, even tone and may speak in a quiet voice that isn't overpowering. Their response time to a question is often slow, and pauses inserted before each of their spoken sentences are not uncommon. When they do speak, they use feeling language.

Why Are Your Eyes Closed?

A Class President business coach relayed a story to me about the first time she consulted with an Activist potential client.

The first telling point was when the Activist reached out to hold the Class President's hand.

Once they reached the point in the conversation where it was time to discuss the fees and commit to the working relationship, there was another surprise.

The Activist started crying, closed her eyes, and kept them shut.

The silence continued.

At first the Class President was concerned and wondered if the price had caused a medical reaction.

It turned out the Activist was just going inside to see if this decision felt right.

After the "check-in" happened, the sale was successfully made, and the Class President learned to allow that space for her Activist clients.

Activists are the least likely to speak over others in conversation. They are also the most likely to speak in new age terms, with their language expressing their personal beliefs and concerns for the environment, equality, or other cause.

Psyche

If we are to understand ourselves and others, we must first understand how driving needs impact our lives. The four driving needs that influence the majority of our decisions are *certainty*, *variety*, *significance*, and *connection*.

Business Travel: Class President Versus Activist

Contributed by John H.

As entrepreneurs, my wife and I will frequently travel for business. My wife has a lot of Class President in her, and I have a lot of Activist in me.

The first thing I should say is that we both love traveling, but we express that love in different ways. I'll never forget when we relocated across America for our careers.

Being an Activist, I thought we were going to enjoy the long journey every step of the way. We'd probably be spellbound by the natural beauty of our country and then slowly discuss our feelings, right?

After all, we were going to be in a car for days, driving and looking out the windows. As I turned to her and asked her about what she thought of the majestic West Virginia mountains gleaming in the new morning sun, I was struck dumb.

She was sleeping!

It turns out my Class President wife likes the *arriving* part of travel, and as an Activist, I like the *getting there* part.

Driving Need

The Activist's driving need is for connection. This means experiencing someone's humanity, vulnerability, and heart. Activists desire to feel that attachment with the people they meet and are looking to feel at peace with everyone. Not as in "world peace," although that may rank high on their list, but peace as in a calmness, comfort, and assurance in their day-to-day life.

For some Activists, this comes from having been exposed to chaos or uncertainty when they were younger and the consequent desire to avoid it as an adult. The need for assurance and peace can sometimes hold Activists back and make them averse to risk. That is part of why they move at a slower pace and are not at all impulsive. They don't like the unknown and don't appreciate change.

More important than financial wealth, achievement, or other material needs, the driving need for Activists is the need for connection. Above all other things, Activists desire to be understood and accepted for who they really are. That is when they feel the most connected to another person.

Character Traits

Activists are nurturing individuals who are accepting of others and provide them with a great deal of emotional support. Well-balanced Activists are good communicators and sensitive to the feelings of others. If not well balanced, the Activist may be overly sensitive to the point of paralyzing action or progress.

Activists can struggle when it comes to accomplishing goals, simply because they are more people oriented and less task oriented. Also, Activists aren't looking to place on a leaderboard, and so many of the usual incentive programs you may offer to help people meet goals will not motivate an Activist. Using negative incentives may be mildly effective, but they are just as likely to backfire because an overwhelmed Activist will bow out if he or she feels too pressured.

An Activist is typically uncomfortable with public acknowledgment and prefers to celebrate his or her wins privately or in an intimate setting. The Activist enjoys being part of a community, doesn't necessarily enjoy traditional sports, and believes in cooperation over competition. The Activist is the Character Code most likely to participate in community or co-op experiences that are focused on doing good for society or take part in cooperative living such as sharing expenses or resources. Many are drawn to the outdoors and feel connected to nature.

A healthy Activist can be very nurturing and supportive of others and will hold a safe space for them. Other people may feed off their calm and loving acceptance. Activists can benefit from learning more organizational skills and systems to help them to manage tasks and to follow through with consistency. Sometimes they resist technology, and in today's world of social media and Internet marketing, that resistance can be just an excuse they'll use to hold themselves back.

The Inner Meanie

The Activists' inner meanie tells them they are not capable. Depending on their ability to deal with this internal message, they may avoid anything new in their lives for fear they are not up to the challenge.

Some Activists beat themselves up for not being like the faster-paced Character Codes around them. These other Character Codes may get things accomplished much faster and are comfortable taking risks, thus earning quicker rewards. So the Activists' inner meanie tells them they aren't that talented or brave or capable, which prevents them from taking action. It is much better for the Activists to realize that their way of looking at the world comes naturally and to focus on doing what they do best without comparison.

Access the resource "Taming the Activist Meanie" for tips and insight (and a little humor) at http://charactercode.com/activistmeanie.

Conflict, Stress, and Emotions

Activists don't like conflict. They may be too compliant, just to avoid a confrontation. Sometimes they get pushed around or walked over by other Character Codes who aren't as sensitive. The empowered Activist creates an environment of understanding, nurturing, and cooperation. However, in challenge an Activist may lack backbone and allow others to overlook or take advantage of them.

Activists are primarily interested in emotions, and so at times they can be overly sensitive. In my opinion, sensitivity training in the workplace is an idea created for Activists to influence the overly blunt Class President or Actor.

Activists can be good at letting you know how they feel, especially if you provide a safe environment in which they can open up. If not, they may just tell you what you want to hear or hide their feelings to avoid conflict. But Activists must be careful to avoid giving away their power simply to avoid confrontation. If they are perceived as acquiescent, they are vulnerable to bullying. That is when resentment creeps in and may lead to passive-aggressive behavior on the part of an upset Activist that didn't speak up.

Health and Wellness

The Activist tends to be interested in preventive health and alternative care. This is the Character Code most likely to see a naturopath or practice homeopathy. Health choices run the gamut from chiropractic to colonics to flower therapy and more.

When you go to a restaurant, Activists are prone to issue the most complicated order, giving instructions to avoid dairy or gluten or other food allergens. They are interested in caring for their bodies and the planet and often invest a great deal of time and energy in learning more about these subjects.

Whether or not you share these interests, Activists appreciate your respectful consideration of who they are. We all deserve to feel acceptance and respect. The quickest way to alienate the Activist is to make fun of or negate something about which he or she feels passionately. Some of the less sensitive Character Codes can easily do this and are unaware of the damage they cause in another human being's psyche.

Jobs and Careers

The Activist's greatest joy is connecting with and getting to know people, most often through listening, talking, or caring for others. As a result, they often work in healing or with children or animals. Many people in counseling, social work, nonprofits, animal rescue, and spiritual professions are Activists, largely in response to the passion, sacrifice, and people skills required for those jobs.

Activists can be great team players, but if they are working with a bunch of Class Presidents or Actors, their slower pace will drive these colleagues crazy. Activists are often repelled by the behavior of Class Presidents and Actors, whom they view as aggressive and insensitive. Although Activists may not like conflict or confrontation, they can often be a calming and peacekeeping force of nature in business relationships.

125

Since Activists like people and often work in the holistic or healing arts, they may spend a great deal of time talking about the life-changing benefits of their work. They could benefit from editing what they say to shorten the description and increase the clarity. Learning to focus on the results and clearly describing their process is also a needed skill.

Many Activists are doing work they love but are struggling with being paid at the level that matches their worth and value. They aren't naturally competitive or ambitious, and some are shy about asking for money for doing the work they love. Of course, learning to request reasonable compensation is simply a skill that can be mastered with some thoughtful work and support from others.

Marketing and Sales

Activists can't stand anyone who seems "salesy." Activists want authenticity and genuineness in all their activities. If you want to reach them in your marketing efforts, you must understand their dreams and fears. They want to serve humanity, not struggle for money, and have a lifestyle that allows them to move at their own pace and participate in the activities they love.

More than likely, the greatest fear for Activists is being thrown into a strange, unknown environment where they are asked to give an impromptu speech pitching some kind of offer or proposal in front of a crowd. That's a mix of many things that would make an Activist uncomfortable; he or she would likely run from the room if asked to do it. An Activist's nightmare would be feeling rushed, pushed, disconnected, and misunderstood.

Activists are unlikely salespeople unless they have a passion for their product. If they do, they may talk way too long and are too verbose in their presentation. If you are a speaker addressing a crowd of Activists, you must acknowledge them as a whole and create an experience that engages their mind, body, and spirit.

When marketing to an Activist, think in terms of natural, organic, sustainable, local, fair trade, noncorporate, and so forth. Attractive colors can run the gamut from earthy to vibrant. You can go with a calming look or a probing, healthful, even soulful look.

What problems can you help Activists solve? You could, for example, provide solutions that help them deal with time management, get organized, handle technology, or attract clients. Make sure your message is low key, is in alignment with who you are, and feels welcoming to your ideal client!

When it comes to deciding to make a purchase or becoming your client, Activists definitely weigh their decisions carefully. They also place value on their intuition, may utilize group consensus, or may consult their support network before deciding to take action.

The Ideal Client

For an Activist, any work or learning experience is better when the whole person is considered. If the Activist is your ideal client, consider not just your content, but also the aesthetics and comfort of the physical space in which you put the Activist.

The Activist's ideal environment may involve a sacred circle of nurturing along with beautiful, soulful music. An Activist craves acceptance and understanding. Therefore, the first impression you make with an Activist client must show you are an authentic, caring, and genuine person. Anticipate a longer sales cycle.

Build systems and contingencies into your business that provide reassurance and nurturing along the way. It will also help your Activist clients if you can track their progress and provide consistent feedback and community.

When you have a relationship with a nurturing and accepting Activist, you will be surprised at how good you feel whenever you are around him or her. I think this is why so many Activists are therapists; they understand how to create a safe space.

That said, the Activist prefers to be around other Activists more than any other Character Code. Activists may also be drawn to Artists and some Cheerleaders if they aren't too much of a whirlwind or move too fast. Activists are least compatible with Actors.

Only select Activists as your ideal clients if you are a patient person, feel a connection, can speak their language, respect their beliefs, and honor them for who they are.

Summarizing the Activist

If you are the Activist, or at least it's one of your top two Character Codes, you can work on developing a greater belief in yourself and the ability to express yourself confidently. I believe Character Coding can really empower you in this regard. When you notice that inner meanie whispering you aren't as capable, fast, savvy, techie, or whatever enough, remind yourself this meanie is just part of being an Activist. Every Character Code has a meanie, as well as a gift to offer, and the Activist is just as special as any of the rest.

Advice for the Activist

If you are frustrated, discouraged, or resentful, remind yourself: this is just a feeling and not a true reflection of who you are. The way you do things has real value, and I'm a big believer in playing to your strengths. Activists often overlook this fact. Therefore, make a list with two columns, one labeled "strengths" and the other "challenges." On the strengths side, list everything in which you excel. Include everything, from your abilities to your feelings. On the challenges side, list the things you struggle with, both activities and feelings. For everything in the challenge column, find a way to involve someone else in your life who can help with those areas or come up with a system for how to handle those challenges. Be patient and kind with yourself as you work on this. Be willing to give yourself a longer timeline for the challenge column. Then structure your life and career around the strengths so you can be a shining star.

This is a good plan for all the Character Codes. If we were all good at doing everything, life would be boring and so would we. Be gentle with yourself when you know you are operating outside your strengths. It is my hope that the Character Code System gives you that permission.

Advice for Interacting with Activists

If you aren't an Activist but your ideal client is, you need to consider the visual and verbal message you must send to communicate effectively with him or her. An Activist desires to be authentic and is emotionally vulnerable. When Activists see you, they need to know you are safe. This is especially important if you are speaking on a topic outside their comfort zone.

Imagine you are a social media expert speaking to a room of holistic health practitioners. Make sure your Activist audience is comfortable asking you questions. State that it is totally acceptable to ask any questions about using social media technology. You would lose your audience if you focused solely on the technical jargon and the logistics behind launching a blog. However, if you described the benefits of creating an online community and how it's a great way to share your message and gift with the world, then you are talking your audience's language. Don't make Activists sit and listen the whole time. Figure out how to make it physical by moving about and taking regular breaks.

Review the "Appearance," "Presentation," and "Speaking" sections and consider adding some of those items to your look and behavior in order to connect with the Activist crowd. Always be true to who you are and see what little things you can add to make your ideal client comfortable. Your objective is making sure your message lands with your audience.

Be reassuring and genuine. If your beliefs are in alignment, you can use the same spirit language. However, don't fake it. You must be real. Make sure to determine that the Activist is your ideal client and then have effective systems in place for working with this Character Code.

First Impressions with the Activist

When meeting an Activist for the first time, be aware of the way you express your body. Hold eye contact, be engaging, listen, and take the time to respond to what the other person actually says. If you appear dishonest or if you seem rigid, either physically or in your thinking, it will be a turnoff. Don't move too fast, don't be pushy, and don't try a hard sell or use scare tactics. Be willing to hug, or at least be warm and outgoing, and take the time to really get to know people.

If this is really difficult for your Character Code, consider your time with an Activist as a healing interaction for you to grow into. You may be surprised. You may find spending time with your Activist friends is when you get to be your most real and true self. Or they may just drive you nuts. Be open to discovering what might work. If it doesn't work out, you can always pick a different Character Code.

Here are some things you can do to add to your look that put an Activist at ease:

>> Select jewelry that is earthy or has natural stones, such as quartz.

>> Look pulled together, but not perfect.

>> Wear layered sweaters instead of a suit.

>> Be willing to maintain eye contact.

>> Speak personally and share your struggles and humanity.

Here are some elements of a first impression that make an Activist wary:

>> You look flawless with everything done perfectly.

>> You have really high hair with excessive hairspray and heavy makeup (i.e., you look like an Actor).

>> You move really fast, talk over others, interrupt, and don't actively listen.

>> You exhibit thinking and language that is black or white, right versus wrong.

If the Activist is your ideal client, be careful with the use of urgent language, deadlines, and incentives. While those are important marketing tools, the Activist can become overwhelmed and turned off with too much pressure or speed. Activists need to feel nurtured and supported throughout the process. When they do make the decision to work with you or participate in some new adventure, they're going to consider how it will affect everything: body, mind, and spirit. If you are able to show that you, your product or your program will support all these aspects, there will be a better connection.

One of the Activist's greatest strengths is being able to connect deeply with people. That's why Activists often serve as the neutral ground, buffer, or calming force in group dynamics. You can count on them to be loyal and supportive.

How to Read a Client Now

Now that you have read the Activist Character Code in detail, you'll want to remember to:

» Begin your "people watching" with new eyes and see how many Activists you can find.

» Notice how the driving need for connection dictates the Activist's behavior and appearance and start identifying the patterns you see.

» Consider if the Activist is the right ideal Character Code client for you.

» Observe what, if any, changes you would need to make in your personal branding to make sure you can communicate with the Activist.

» Begin to feel more compassion for Activists (or yourself) when you consider their inner meanie and what you learned in the "Psyche" section.

In Chapter 8 you will learn how to identify an Artist Character Code. This will include all the details you need to better communicate with, connect to, attract, and read Artists from across the room.

Take the following action steps now:

» Download the "Activist Character Code Overview" to have the details and color sketches right at your fingertips at http://charactercode.com/activist.

» Access the resource "Taming the Activist Meanie" for tips and insight (and a little humor) at http://charactercode.com/activistmeanie.

EIGHT

The Artist Character Code

Fight to Be Free

THE NEXT CHARACTER Code is called the Artist because I wanted you to get a picture in your head of someone that is a free thinker—you can think of Artists as operating to the beat of their own drum. Artists have a driving need for significance, which they most often serve through creative self-expression.

Unlike the Actor, however, they do not enjoy the spotlight. It is an interesting mix of wanting to be seen as a unique individual but not wanting to attract too much attention. These two desires are often at odds with one another.

Artists have some similarities to the Activist and many key differences. One of the things that set Artists apart is their fashion choices, which are always interesting, eclectic, and highly individualistic. As a result, Artists are very easy to identify. Many fashion designers are Artists.

Artists can switch between being people oriented and task oriented and tend to move at a slower pace than the other Character Codes. As you read about the Artist's appearance, presentation, and speaking style, you'll see how much the Artist's driving need for significance influences each of these categories. Are you an Artist? Do you know any people who are Artists? Let's jump in so you can learn how to read them from across the room.

Appearance

The things we care most about are reflected in our appearance, and we are constantly giving clues to others about how we want to be treated.

Hair

The Artist will likely have a very stylized haircut. Women of this Character Code often sport a short, spiky hairdo. The female Artist may have her hair dyed a dark black or maroon or have one thick streak of blond, blue, or pink—something that sets her apart from the crowd. Most Artists will have a well-groomed look in whatever distinctive style they select. They are also likely to change their hairstyles or colors frequently.

If you ever see a guy with a pompadour, it's likely he's an Artist. Artist men are also more likely to have facial hair in a variety of styles, from retro sideburns to a trendy soul patch. Some Artists are more flamboyant and use feathers, braids, or hair jewelry to demonstrate their individuality and creativity.

Both men and women Artists can range from having a really bold hairstyle, such as a Mohawk, to exhibiting a more conservative look, such as a dark dye with a precision asymmetrical cut that could pass in many work environments and yet still show their distinct style. They will typically use hair products daily and be well versed in hair care.

Makeup

The Artist woman will often wear natural makeup and be more experimental with her eye makeup than the other Codes. Occasionally she will use dark lipstick; however, smoky eye shadow and a dark eyeliner are more common. An Artist will often change her look.

Many teens wearing clothing in the Gothic style are Artists. This Character Code's makeup often becomes less dramatic as an adult. Many men who wear eyeliner are often Artists.

Jewelry

Jewelry for Artist women is best described as an interesting collection of individual items combined to create a unique, creative look. Artists have spread the message that we're all supposed to be eclectic in our fashion choices—that fashion means selecting items that are not part of a matching set. When you look at each item, it is different and has its own character. That's how Artists wear their jewelry and other accessories. Observers often think, "I never would have thought to put all those items together. How did she know how to make that work?"

This is important for Artists, but not for other Character Codes, because it is part of how Artists demonstrate their creativity. Artists are likely to experiment with mixing metals, other materials, and genres to achieve their look. It isn't uncommon to see them wearing different-length necklaces, unusual rings, and a wide-cuff bracelet with a buckle.

Artist men also experiment with their jewelry and often wear more than many other men. An Artist is the Character Code most likely to have piercings, wear disc or gauge earrings (stretching your earlobe with an oversized hole), and have tattoos.

Clothing

Artists will continue their eclectic look with their clothing, and both men and women may choose to shop in vintage stores. They are typically fashion conscious and enjoy standing out from everyone else. They often avoid the popular trends or just use a part of a trend and put their unique spin on it. They are more likely to pull from past trends that are no longer fashionable and reinvent the look.

Artists lean toward creating multiple looks, intermixing a range of historical time periods, previous fads, or cultures. Some Artists show up in what looks like wearable art, or at the very least, an ensemble crafted with a creative eye. They may create an interesting color palette such as combining turquoise with orange or pink with yellow.

Some Artists will create one look they love, which becomes their trademark. Fashion choices may range from runway dramatic to an oversized dress shirt to torn jeans, but whatever the look is, they'll make it their own.

Accessories

Artists often won't carry a purse, or if they do, it is likely a stylized work of art. Some Artist women may carry a tiny box purse—for example, one that looks like a Chinese food takeout container with elaborate designs in silk. Others may carry large bags or perhaps a beaded vintage clutch. It is about the purse being part of the outfit, not about its utility.

Artist men often carry a messenger bag over one shoulder. They too are looking for an accessory that completes their look. If they are required to carry a briefcase, it would be very contemporary, stylish, and cool. Artists definitely prefer fashion over function!

Eye-Catching in Blue

One of the things I love about summer is attending local farmers' markets. Besides all the fresh food, I enjoy seeing the family-run businesses operate and sell their goods.

After you attend a few farmers' markets, they start to all feel the same. The stalls and many of the owners have a similar look and sound.

So imagine my surprise one day as I strolled up the middle aisle of the market to see a very large crowd gathered around one vendor's stall. I drew near to see what the appeal was.

What I saw was an Artist serving her homemade bakery goods to a rush of happy clients.

The Artist had blue hair, a retro 1950s dress, and a complete persona branded in her signage and labels around her bakery booth.

It didn't matter that at least four other vendors were selling bread in her aisle alone—she stood out.

People talked about her blue hair and baked goods. They started to follow her from one farmers' market to another, generating enough traction that she opened her first store and continues to expand.

Don't hide who you are—use it in your branding!

Nails

An Artist's nails are typically a dark shade or not done at all. It would be rare to see an Artist with nails painted in candy pink. Artists don't usually have long nails or spend time in salons, preferring to care for their own nails.

Some Artist men will wear nail polish, with the darker shades being the most popular. Occasionally you'll see an Artist man or woman with blue, green, or other atypical nail color.

Shoes

The shoes of female Artists can range from heels to sandals to boots, and they're likely to own a lot of them. Shoes are often their main fashion statement, particularly if there is a required dress code that limits their expression at work. Female Artists will sport shoe colors that other Character Codes would not wear. As far as styles go, you will see everything from a dramatic stiletto to wide platforms to a pointy-toed heel to a vintage Mary Jane pump.

The male Artist will also express his unique style in his footwear, ranging from hip sneakers to Doc Martens to saddle shoes to vintage wing tips.

Presentation

Artists project a demeanor of being too cool for words. This can create a barrier in getting to know them. They will enter a room and find that their polished and eclectic appearance sets them apart from the group or makes them seem aloof. The Artists receive this feedback from others, and that just widens the distance between them. This fuels the belief (and fear) by Artists that they are different from everyone else. The very thing that makes Artists feel unique (their appearance) is also the thing that keeps them apart from most people.

As a result of a lifetime of these experiences, Artists will hang around the fringe of a group, carefully observing before making a move. They will behave in a cautious manner. They are unlikely to speak loudly, be pushy, or take control of the room.

Now that you know this about Artists, you can take the first step in approaching them. Once they get over their initial skepticism, you will break through that barrier and quickly find a friend.

Speaking

Artists are listeners; however, they are listeners with their own distinct opinions. They are creatively minded and express this in their language. Artists are thoughtful, capable, and interested in deep thinking. They talk in an even and measured tone that allows time for processing the information. They often seem a little reserved or reluctant when you initially meet them. Once they know they can trust you, they will freely express their opinions and feelings.

Artists usually have a variety of opinions regarding music, politics, and spirituality, and they are open to discuss each topic—often passionately—when the opportunity arises. They enjoy actively engaging in debate on any of these topics or other subjects that many other Character Codes would avoid. Artists dislike small talk and mindless chitchat and would rather discuss weighty topics of social or international significance.

An Opinionated Debate

Contributed by Jennifer D.

One time I was at a dinner party sitting next to my friend Dan. I'm an Artist, and he is the ultimate Scholar. We started talking about poor people. I said I believe society should take care of poor people. Share the wealth.

Dan is convinced that rich people have the right to keep all their money and not share any of it. He has every fact and figure to prove it, but his recitation of it all was dry as a bone.

For every point I brought up, he had some fact to refute it. I was desperate to get it through his thick skull that wealth spread, through services like healthcare and schools, provides better living for us all.

Dan would not have any of it.

I don't care if people disagree with me. I welcome it and the discussion that ensues. Dan did not share my feelings about our debate. He has, according to him, dissected every possible truth. In the end he was annoyed with me, and now he won't talk to me because I did not see how right he was.

I just enjoyed the lively discussion!

Artists love adjectives and expressive verbs. They often use colorful and descriptive language in their writing and speaking. They tend to have a well-developed vocabulary and be well read. They often evoke emotional responses and vivid mental images in the listener as they speak.

Psyche

When your client's driving need is met—for example, through your selling or marketing—you can expect a positive outcome.

Driving Need

Artists have a driving need for significance, without the spotlight. They want to be recognized as an individual—someone who is special, creative, and one-of-a-kind—but they aren't looking to be the center of attention. Like the Activists, the Artists appreciate connection, but it is their drive for uniqueness that sets them apart and initiates their lifestyle choices.

The bottom line is that Artists almost always feel different from those around them. Of course, all people feel like this from time to time, but Artists and Actors experience it the most. Artists choose the manner and degree that they are going to express that feeling of difference. It may be demonstrated by their creative choices in dress or lifestyle, or it may be displayed in an extreme and dramatic way that will serve to alienate others.

For some Artists, this driving need for significance comes from having been overlooked as a child. Some Artists may have come from a large family and didn't feel they received enough individual attention. Or they may not have shared the same Character Code as the majority of their family members or community, and that made them feel alienated.

Character Traits

Once you get past that initial barrier of inaccessibility, you'll find Artists to be passionate, nurturing, and loyal friends. They can be very supportive of you and very tolerant of differences in others.

We're Looking for a Few Good Artists

It is great when businesses realize that they can use Character Coding not just for attracting clients but also for finding the right employees.

I watched one company have this realization and change its method of hiring along with its corporate environment. The company wanted to attract animation artists, graphic designers, and creative and hip minds.

Turns out they were looking for a few good Artists!

They bent the traditional corporate rules to create a work environment that allowed their employees to set their own hours—occasionally working from home or working late hours in the office, such as a noon to 8 p.m. shift.

The corporate dress code was lifted; the internal offices were redesigned to bring in game stations, areas to inspire creative thinking and play, and healthy food; and policy was changed to to give individual employees the freedom to decorate their own work space as they wished.

The work was demanding, and the environment was fun, creative, and inspiring. It became a beacon and natural magnet for Artists as one of the best places to work.

Oddly, because their appearance is often unique, many people assume Artists are judgmental. Not so. Because Artists regard themselves as different, they tolerate differences in others; rarely are they judgmental. In fact, they are the most accepting and tolerant of all the Character Codes.

That is not necessarily true of others when encountering an Artist. It is important for Artists to be aware of the assumptions others make about them whenever they enter a new group or speak in front of a crowd. Artists want to be mindful of their audience so they don't alienate them.

Artists desire to be understood and accepted for who they really are. They are willing to fight for the underdog. They aren't competitive and prefer to create a project on their own, though they also appreciate creative collaboration.

Unlike Actors, Artists don't usually like public acknowledgment for themselves, but they do want to be recognized for their unique work, gifts, and talents. It's an interesting mixture of "Don't pay too much attention to me" and "Oh, by the way, please notice that I'm different and unique."

Because they are more concerned with their own significance and individuality, Artists must be careful about losing out on the personal connection with other people, something they know matters to them. Most people usually connect over things they have in common, and then as they get to know each other, they learn to appreciate their differences. Artists focus on the differences from the start and would benefit from noticing the commonalities they have with the people they meet.

The Inner Meanie

The Artists' inner meanie tells them they're not special—and, of course, this is exactly the thing they most fear, being ordinary, lacking talent or a unique purpose. Depending on their tolerance for dealing with this meanie, they may be working overtime to display their individuality through self-expression and activity. Left unresolved, it will create a mild feeling of malcontent or one of total rebellion in extreme.

Some Artists beat themselves up for not being satisfied with the status quo. It's better for Artists to realize this is part of what makes them special and just appreciate their gift. They will always be a voice for creativity and often equality and other civil rights. Artists are great at championing the unseen victor in us all.

Access the resource "Taming the Artist Meanie" for tips and insight (and a little humor) at http://charactercode.com/artistmeanie.

Conflict, Stress, and Emotions

Well-adjusted Artists can be very supportive of others, allowing for their differences and creating a safe space for those differences to be expressed. Sometimes when I think of this, I picture the old beat-nik poetry bars, or some of the Renaissance painters, or any group throughout history known for its deep thinking and feelings about self-expression, freedom, and personal significance.

A less well-adjusted Artist will be argumentative and always looking for a debate. He or she will easily pick fights or create con-tention. Depending on how the Artist is feeling, he or she can be the force that creates division in groups or unites them. The Artist seeks freedom and often disdains playing by society's rules or following a cookie-cutter lifestyle.

When Artists are upset, they have to be mindful about isolating themselves and just retreating from the group or source of conflict.

Health and Wellness

Some Artists may neglect their health, and in extreme cases, they may abuse their body with drugs or drinking, such as some musicians or other creative types that feel tormented or lost in life. On the milder side, Artists may use cigarette smoking, caffeine, or other stimulants as a way to set themselves apart from the crowd and feed their need for significance. Watch an Artist order an espresso or cappuccino and see how specific the order can be.

Some Artists have swung to the opposite extreme and become very health conscious, typically opting for alternative therapies or care. In this situation they may use their knowledge, opinions, and freedom of choice regarding their health to demonstrate they are dis-cerning and not just following the masses.

Jobs and Careers

Artists who are not well adjusted can strain group dynamics and even some corporate environments. Well-adjusted Artists are a welcome addition to the group because they bring original insight and creativ-ity to the table. They can add a fresh perspective to a conservative or staid work culture.

Many Artists seek jobs in creative professions—everything from design, fashion, computers, entertainment, and writing. Examples of jobs would include painters, fashion designers, chefs, or other creative hands-on people that may shy away from using technology. Other Artists, such as graphic designers and animation artists, are very tech savvy.

Many Artists are doing work they love, but some struggle with getting paid what they are worth. Some Artists work through their money issues, while others struggle, needing deeper work, depending on the level of mistrust and conspiracy theory the current culture inspires in them.

Artists can benefit from learning how to quickly build rapport with a group and monetize doing what they love.

Marketing and Sales

Artists are completely turned off by people who come across as "salesy," seem unreal, or lack original thinking. Artists want authenticity and genuineness in all their activities and friends.

An Artist's fear is being forced to live in a housing development filled with cookie-cutter homes, prefurnished with particleboard shelving, ruled by an implied dress code, and surrounded by people of the same race, careers, politics, or religious beliefs. An Artist would feel stifled and crave to break free for some self-expression. This is why Artists prefer to make highly personalized choices in products, services, and programs, which are often tailored to them. An Artist who is part of a community would want it to be full of many *individuals*.

Artists typically require a longer sales cycle. They appreciate business systems that allow for choice and customization. If you make offers to groups or run mass campaigns to generate clients and Artists are your target audience, it's important to emphasize that your product or program can be individually tailored for them. This doesn't mean you have to provide a custom service for every client, but it's important for Artists to know you have two or three choices from which to select.

The Artists' dream may involve a vibrant, diverse community of creative individuals with open minds. They crave significance, meaning, and the need to be understood. The Artist's nightmare is feeling unappreciated, stereotyped, overlooked, or otherwise diminished. If you are addressing a crowd of Artists, acknowledge them as individuals.

When marketing to an Artist, go out of your way to be creative. An Artist will be attracted to your eclectic, pulled-together look. Good colors for an Artist would be any combination that looks original and hip. If what you're offering is too busy, looks salesy, or looks like a boring template, Artists will be turned off. Make sure your message conveys individuality, creativity, and passion for your work.

Artists' problems often center on managing a business, monetizing their work, and understanding how to market themselves and their work. For example, you could provide solutions to help them deal with monetizing their passion or their creative work, break through that initial contact and connect with their clients, navigate the cookie-cutter world, or handle conflict.

When it comes to deciding to make a purchase or become your client, Artists weigh their decision carefully and appreciate individual work and attention. If Artists are your ideal clients, realize they will want to connect with you first and want to be assured you know who they are, that you "get" them.

The Ideal Client

If the Artist is your ideal client, it is essential that you make a first impression that shows you are an authentic, caring, and genuine person who recognizes your client is a unique, creative individual. Artists want to feel significant and understood. They want to know that they are not being judged or overlooked.

If you provide custom work, a customized product, or individualized time, then the Artist might be a great ideal Character Code client. Feature this ability to individualize as a benefit in your marketing. Artists will appreciate support, accountability, and a community of open-minded individuals. If your service offers an ongoing program, your Artists may disappear from the scene from time to time. It will be helpful if you can build tracking and varying levels of engagement into your business model. These are not the people that you want to send a faceless, mass-produced direct-mail message to.

The Artist prefers to be around other Artists more than any other Character Codes. Artists also like being with Activists and are the most tolerant of all the Character Codes, often finding it interesting or intriguing to observe the differences in people. The Artist is the one best suited to handle a difficult Actor.

Summarizing the Artist

If you are the Artist, or it is at least one of your top two Character Codes, you can start by having a greater belief in yourself as a special and unique individual whose qualities do not require proof. When you notice that inner meanie speaking negatively about how you aren't special, remind yourself that this is just part of being an Artist—your inner meanie can take the night off. Everyone has inherent value, and you are unique without having to always set yourself apart. Even in a uniform, you would be unique.

Advice for the Artist

If you are feeling alone, misunderstood, and different from everyone else, it is time to get out there and start connecting with other people. Approach them and begin the discussion. Look for what you have in common instead of just focusing on the differences.

You will find that your feelings and ideas aren't so unusual, that we all struggle to find meaning and purpose in life. The differences you do notice are part of what makes you unique, and your ability to accept others is one of the gifts you offer the world.

Advice for Interacting with Artists

If you aren't an Artist but your ideal client is, you need to consider the visual and verbal message you must send in order to communicate effectively. Artists will feel more of a connection if you can reflect back some of what they appreciate. Keep in mind the Artists' greatest fears. Make sure you don't set up your office, product, or event to mirror that fear. The type of atmosphere, materials, image, and language you would create for a group of attorneys or realtors would be entirely different from what you would do for Artists.

Review the "Appearance," "Presentation," and "Speaking" sections and personalize some of those items to hone your look and behavior so you can effectively connect, but bear in mind that Artists are not concerned with you matching them. It's always best to be true to who you are and just show up as the shiny version of you.

Make sure to evaluate if the Artist is the ideal client for you and then have effective systems in place for working with this Character Code.

First Impressions with the Artist

When meeting an Artist for the first time, be aware of your appearance and presentation. Be attentive, look him or her in the eye, listen well, and respond to what is actually said. Just like the Activist, don't move too fast, don't be pushy, and don't try too hard to sell or use scare tactics.

Some Artists aren't into hugging, and some are; it should be obvious by their body language. It will be a turnoff if you appear fake or unoriginal in your own thinking and opinions. Artists often prefer creative language rather than business language. Artists like to use adjectives and other descriptive terms.

Here are some things you can do to enhance your first impression that put an Artist at ease:

>> Wear accessories that are creative, unique, original, and eye-catching.

>> Go for an eclectic look—avoid looking too much like a businessperson.

>> Show an appreciation for fashion and things that are aesthetically pleasing.

>> Hold eye contact and engage in an actual discussion, not just small talk.

>> Have your own opinion and ideas.

What is off-putting to an Artist?

>> You have a cookie-cutter image, offer a conventional message, or display a one-size-fits-all mentality.

>> You don't pay attention to your image or self-expression.

>> You move really fast, talk over everyone, interrupt, or don't actively listen.

>> You placate on every issue and speak in clichés.

If you have a business service or product that provides a new or unique approach—something off the beaten path—then the Artist might be an ideal client. Your marketing and sales department would find it creatively stimulating to conceive of the original and hip campaign required to capture the Artist's attention.

One of the Artist's greatest strengths is seeing someone else's individuality and allowing it to be. That's part of why Artists are often found in creative circles. Do the same for them, and they will feel an affinity with you.

How to Read a Client Now

Now that you have read the Artist Character Code in detail, you'll want to remember to:

» Begin your "people watching" with new eyes and see how many Artists you can find.

» Notice how the driving need for significance dictates the Artist's behavior and appearance and start identifying the patterns you see.

» Consider if the Artist is the ideal Character Code client for you.

» Observe what, if any, changes you would need to make in your personal branding to make sure you can communicate with the Artist.

» Begin to feel more compassion for Artists (or yourself) when you consider their inner meanie and what you learned in the "Psyche" section.

In Chapter 9 you will learn which Character Codes get along and which clash. This will help you to better understand the group dynamics in the workplace and in your personal life and will also help you make better decisions in choosing those work and personal relationships.

Take the following action steps now:

» Download the "Artist Character Code Overview" to have the details and color sketches right at your fingertips at http://charactercode.com/artist.

» Access the resource "Taming the Artist Meanie" for tips and insight (and a little humor) at http://charactercode .com/artistmeanie.

NINE

Which Character Codes Get Along and Which Clash?

Choosing Your Relationships in Business and Life

NOW THAT YOU'VE read about each of the Character Codes and learned that you are a Class President, does it mean you should avoid all Activists? Or if you've discovered you're a Cheerleader, does it mean you can't work with a Scholar?

Not necessarily.

As you learned in Chapter 1, it's important to be able to identify all the Character Codes. You'll want to develop relationships with some, and others you'll prefer to avoid. Personal benefits abound as well, because you'll learn not to take certain behaviors in others personally and will be more understanding and compassionate about their differences.

Character Codes Connections

In business, these deeper perceptions about which Character Codes get along and which don't are often useful in identifying your perfect business partner, ideal client, and target market; in resolving human resource conflicts; and in seeking many other creative solutions. Here are the basics to get you started.

The Class President Character Code

The *Class President* Character Code typically prefers the company of other *Class Presidents*. Class Presidents need to avoid getting into a competitive relationship or "one-upping" each other. Yet two balanced and supportive Class Presidents can form a dynamic partnership.

Class Presidents often get along well with *Cheerleaders* because both are fast paced and upbeat. At times the Cheerleader's lack of follow-through or practice of bouncing from one idea to another irritates the Class President. Conversely, Cheerleaders are often able to get the Class Presidents to loosen up and have more fun.

Class Presidents tend to avoid *Actors*. Class Presidents often feel that Actors are just too dramatic or apt to blurt out inappropriate things. Actors bring out the more conservative nature of the Class President. Class Presidents in business are wary of the Actor's hyperbole and may be judgmental. However, an Actor can sometimes get a Class President to take more risks.

Class Presidents appreciate the *Scholar's* detached approach, focus on data, and objectivity. The Class President gets irritated with the Scholar's slower pace and perfectionism when those behaviors get in the way of completing tasks. Class Presidents are more likely to want to outsource tasks versus the Scholars' preference to micromanage the details. It can be a good partnership if they each play to their strengths and stay out of each other's areas of expertise. In this type of union between two task-oriented Character Codes, they often need a third person to help bring forth the humanity, vulnerability, and personal touch. A Class President and Scholar working together may easily become too detached and clinical.

Class Presidents get easily frustrated and impatient with *Activists*. Class Presidents feel that an Activist moves too slowly, and they perceive indecision in the Activist's slower style of speech and pauses. These two Character Codes operate at completely different speeds, and everything from physical movement to decision making is night and day for them. Class Presidents often avoid partnerships with Activists. If Class Presidents and Activists understand each other and can accept their differences, it can be a real complementary union, with the Class President handling strategy and the Activist handling the human connection. The Activist can get the Class President to slow down and start feeling.

"You're Messing with My Need for Certainty!"

As a Class President, I've had my share of frustrations working with an Activist assistant. It was his job to handle the setup, sound, and video for my speaking events when I first started out. The work environment and number of variables to manage were too fast paced for his comfort zone. We laugh about it now, but we learned about our differences the hard way.

On one occasion we drove to a speaking engagement 30 minutes away only to discover he had lost the keys to the front door. We were in a near panic trying to figure out how to open the doors as clients began arriving. He drove the hour-long round trip to search for the key, only to realize it had been in the car the entire time. By the time he returned we had hired a locksmith to pick the lock.

During the live events, every time someone was handed the microphone, there was a three- to five-second delay before he reacted and turned on the sound. His reaction time was slow, and it created instant Class President–to–Activist angst.

One time he incorrectly inserted the video memory card during a live event that was only performed one time. It was imperative it be filmed. When the problem was discovered, I had exactly 3 seconds to come up with an activity and improvise for the 60 minutes it took to fix the problem. I had to simultaneously lead from the front of the room and keep things on track and then turn off the microphone during the exercise to try to solve the problem. Mic on, smile and lead the group. Mic off, curse and try to fix the video.

Another time I was onstage in front of hundreds when I saw the entire 40 feet of back wall, piping, and drapery—which he had put up—come crashing down. It was rescued by other assistants just before it hit the floor, and the wall was reconstructed. I had to continue presenting on stage, without flinching or missing a beat, keeping the audience focused up front and not distracted by events in the back of the room.

What were the most important lessons learned from working with this Activist assistant? To expect the unexpected, work on my patience, and use Character Coding in the hiring process. And of course, the perspective is two-sided. The challenges I listed that clearly drove a Class President nuts might just make another Character Code laugh and say, "No big deal!"

Class Presidents are quick to judge the *Artist's* appearance as quirky or offbeat. It isn't a typical partnership, but it has its strengths. The two Character Codes run into pacing issues, and each processes information differently. The relationship works best when the Class President sticks to strategy and the Artist handles creativity. A Class President is more interested in a mass-market approach to business, while an Artist prefers a custom or individualized approach. An Artist can encourage a Class President to notice the finer details.

The Cheerleader Character Code

The *Cheerleader* is often attracted to the *Class President* Character Code. Cheerleaders like the fact that Class Presidents get things done and manage the details. Cheerleaders love being the source of ideas in a business partnership or relationship, without having to actually run the business. A Cheerleader's ideal job might be to wine and dine the clients, attract new deals, and dream up ideas. Sometimes Cheerleaders will be put off by the Class President, complaining that Class Presidents are too demanding, too serious, or too blunt. Class Presidents are great at influencing Cheerleaders to be more mindful of the details, customer service, and follow-through.

The *Cheerleader* loves being around other *Cheerleader* Character Codes. They feed off each other's high energy and enthusiasm. When together, they become animated and loud, laugh a lot, and dream of how successful the business will be. They can inspire and motivate one another to see the big picture and global possibilities. They are glass half-full kind of people. What they often miss when together are the details, reality, and step-by-step process for making it happen. They have a lot of fun but don't necessarily get a lot done. Cheerleaders provide great support for each other because they really understand each other.

Cheerleaders are often attracted to *Actors*. Cheerleaders like the Actor's high energy, power, and charisma. Actors often expose the Cheerleader's naiveté because the Cheerleader will believe every exaggerated claim the Actor makes. Some Cheerleaders feel overpowered by Actors; yet others build a loyal friendship. They have to be careful about becoming competitive or fighting for the spotlight, recognition, or acclaim. An Actor is able to draw out a shy Cheerleader. This duo is more likely to take risks or stay out late at the bar after a work meeting.

Cheerleaders are often totally baffled by *Scholars*. While they may appreciate the Scholar's knowledge, this appreciation comes only after they can get past the Scholar's total disregard and lack of interest in fashion. These two operate at completely different paces and do not speak each other's language: The Cheerleader is all about heart, emotion, energy, and fun, while the Scholar is cerebral, detached, and intellectually methodical. In most work or social settings, these two keep their distance. If they understood one another, a partnership could be formed whereby the Cheerleader handled all the human interaction and acted as the face of the company, leaving the Scholar behind the scenes to manage the operations and details. Ideally, for this arrangement to succeed, they would need a third-party translator or the ability to develop the skills necessary to navigate each other's differences in language, values, and speed.

Cheerleaders and *Activists* typically behave in a very polite, respectful manner toward each other. Each operates at a different pace, however. They are both interested in people, but for different reasons: Activists because they want to connect with the client's humanity and Cheerleaders because gossip is infinitely more interesting than data. Cheerleaders tend to view Activists as too deep or "woo-woo" and won't agree with all their alternative beliefs. Activists encourage Cheerleaders to dig deeper in work and play. As a partnership, this duo is very expressive and great with people but will struggle to get the details done.

Cheerleaders find *Artists* intriguing for their fashion sense and unique style. Cheerleaders will often struggle with the Artist's quirkiness and may feel challenged to find common ground in conversation. Cheerleaders may become frustrated with Artists who nitpick over details and who puzzle over the *why* behind everything when the Cheerleaders just want to have fun. This duo can create conflict when the Artist feels deeply wounded over a wrongdoing and the Cheerleader wants to just gloss over the details and move on.

The Actor Character Code

The *Actor* appreciates the *Class President's* strategic mind and ability to move fast. Sometimes the Actor may be competitive with or perhaps intimidated by the Class President. If the Class President becomes too emotionally removed or clinical, it irritates the Actor. The Class President may be embarrassed by the Actor's grandiose behavior. An outraged Class President and an Actor who feels wronged can produce explosive conflicts. This duo is often at its best when leading others—but not when working together in partnership.

The *Actor* prefers the company of *Cheerleaders* over many other Character Codes. Actors and Cheerleaders operate at similar speeds, share common interests, and like to have fun. Some Actors will consider the Cheerleader too foolish or softhearted. Conflict can arise over sharing the spotlight or expressing emotions and opinions too hastily. This duo works best when the Actor is allowed to lead and the Cheerleader to follow.

The *Actor* typically wants to avoid other *Actors*. In certain business or networking gatherings, you can see them maintain a 12-foot distance between them. They don't like to share the spotlight, and they see another Actor as competition—sometimes even an enemy. If they can forge a friendship and trust one another, they can become powerful allies—but it takes some effort and negotiations to determine who

Don't Get Your Scholars Angry

Contributed by Victoria B.

One of my clients is a very intelligent guy; he holds a PhD in soil chemistry and pesticides. I knew right away that he was a Scholar.

As I began asking him questions about the problem he wanted to solve, he started telling me about his childhood, launching into a detailed account.

After nearly 20 minutes of his stories, the Cheerleader in me was getting restless. As a professional, I knew better than to interrupt, and so I listened attentively and acknowledged his words as he continued the flow of detailed information.

I was waiting for a pause so that I could move us on to the situation at hand, but finally I just broke in and interrupted his story.

He immediately became very angry at me, letting me know that he was not finished.

I tried to get us back on track, as our time was limited. The more I interrupted his train of thought, the angrier he got. Finally, he burst into loud yelling, and his eyes welled up with tears.

I could clearly see that he was very uncomfortable with expressing his feelings and emotions, and I felt at a loss; this wasn't going in the direction that I had hoped.

This was my first lesson in dealing with a Scholar. I now know never to interrupt Scholars, something that Cheerleaders tend to do, when they are giving you a detailed account of a situation or the technical information on how something works.

In the end I was left feeling drained, but my Scholar client had a breakthrough!

gets the accolades. In a typical setting, they will be constantly one-upping and trying to outshine each other.

The *Actor* is typically uninterested in *Scholars*. Actors find Scholars boring, tame, and slow. Scholars are often afraid of Actors. In this partnership the playing fields are not level. Actors will overpower Scholars and may treat them as subservient—as if they were lackeys. This can lead to escalating resentment and passive-aggressive behavior from the Scholar. These two Character Codes are polar opposites when it comes to speed, language, posture, values, and interests.

Holding Court

I knew a woman who was an Actress Character Code. She had a very successful business, traveled extensively, and always had a lot of fun.

She had a larger-than-life personality, and she didn't let aging slow her down or diminish her Actress ways.

She was known to mix business with pleasure—they were one and the same for her. She would often host gatherings that included her clients, her family, and a clown. Then she would hold court during the events and regale us with stories. She always wanted the spotlight—she preferred having all eyes on her.

During one such gathering, I heard the crowd applauding and turned around to find her modeling her newest leopard print lingerie. She waltzed through the living room like it was her own personal runway.

She was in her seventies at the time!

I'm not sure what was funnier, watching this Actress move through the crowd or seeing the expression of absolute mortification on her Class President daughter's face!

The *Actor* typically considers the *Activist* too woo-woo and doesn't understand the Activist's point of view or share the same beliefs. If the Activist is enamored with the Actor and more acquiescing, the Actor will like having the Activist around. In this scenario, the Actor will just disregard or overlook the Activist's preferences. It's tough to get close to an Actor, and so most Activists are unsatisfied in this type of working or personal relationship. It is very common for the Activist to give up power to the Actor in this situation.

The *Actor* is best matched with the *Artist*, not only because of the Actor's preference but because of the Artist's nonjudgmental nature. The Actor considers the Artist quirky but appreciates the Artist's style, creativity, and uniqueness. Both Actors and Artists have a driving need for significance; however, the Actor is looking for the spotlight and the Artist is not, and therefore they complement each another. The Actor always seeks to be the center of attention.

The Scholar Character Code

The *Scholar* appreciates the *Class President's* need for certainty because Scholars have that same driving need themselves. Both like things to be done right, but they have very different styles when it comes to pacing and risk tolerance, which can create conflict. The Scholar believes a task *done right* means done perfectly, whereas the Class President accepts *done well* and checks the task off the list. The Class President can assist the Scholar in taking more risks, moving more quickly, and letting go of "perfect," but it will be an uphill battle. These two Character Codes are also known to focus so intently on tasks that they forget to care for themselves. Working together, they need to be careful not to feed each other's workaholic tendencies.

The *Scholar* is typically intrigued by the ease with which *Cheerleaders* operate in the social world, though Scholars often disregard them in the professional realm. Scholars and Cheerleaders are on opposite extremes in many personality traits. A Cheerleader is able to teach a Scholar a great deal about connecting with people, socializing, networking, and making the interpersonal connection necessary to seal the deal. The challenge lies in getting these two Character Codes to connect and speak the same language. If they are able to allow for each other's differences, they are a dynamic duo where the Cheerleader is the company's face or front person and the Scholar manages and organizes the details.

The *Scholar* will typically shy away—or sometimes run—from an *Actor*. An Actor often projects too much emotion, drama, or energy for the Scholar and that makes the Scholar uncomfortable. Actors can be of great help to Scholars in doing something bold, daring, and outside their comfort zone. That said, it is an unlikely pairing, and most Scholars won't take the risk.

Scholars are naturally drawn to other *Scholars*. Even if they don't share the same interests, they enjoy conversations that showcase each other's expertise. They move at the same speed, have the same predilection for order, and share the same desire to do things right. In a partnership they also have the same challenges, and so the best solution is to have a business that plays to their strengths as a Scholar or join with a third-party to complement them and participate in the social activities for their company.

Blunt

One Scholar reached out to a Class President to discuss a possible business venture in the media realm. The Scholar proceeded to describe her background and experience and to outline what was possible. She ended by saying she was an attorney.

The Class President listening had been quiet the entire time. What were the first words out of her mouth?

"I hate attorneys."

Class Presidents can be a little blunt—or sometimes a lot blunt.

Luckily the Scholar calling liked working with Class Presidents. She loved the woman's directness, and they formed a highly effective business relationship as a result.

When it comes to pacing, *Scholars* often feel drawn to *Activists*. However, Scholars may easily wound Activists by questioning their beliefs (which are feeling and intuitive based) by asking for the facts or proof. If they have a shared interest, it can be a great connection, each learning from the other and coming at problems from entirely different perspectives. Where Activists can help Scholars is in becoming more grounded, getting in touch with their body, and connecting to people. The challenge is getting the Scholar interested in these things.

Scholars find *Artists* intriguing, especially if they are interesting conversationalists on a variety of subjects. Besides other Scholars, the Artist may be one of the few people who will engage the Scholar deeply and will appreciate having someone with whom to discuss topics in which other Character Codes have no interest. The Artist can assist the Scholar in dressing more fashionably and raising the Scholar's image awareness. The Artist may also challenge the Scholar's sense of certainty, which would be healthy but quite a stretch. The two lean toward spending most of their time in their heads, often getting lost in circular thought patterns.

The Activist Character Code

The *Activist* finds the *Class President* demanding and a little intimidating. On one extreme, the Activist views the Class President as bossy, rude, insensitive, and emotionally disconnected. On the other, an Activist may appreciate the Class President's know-how and strategic mindset. These two Character Codes have plenty to argue about when it comes to speed, process, and decision making. They can create a complementary partnership when they understand and learn to appreciate each other. A Class President can encourage an Activist to embrace change and to follow through and complete projects. The Activist can teach the Class President to connect, slow down, and enjoy the moment. Without empathy and understanding, Activists and Class Presidents typically avoid each other in social or work settings and would likely have strong opinions or judgments about each other.

The *Activist* often enjoys the company of *Cheerleaders*. Activists like the Cheerleader's friendly dialogue and easygoing nature and often admire the Cheerleader's adeptness in social situations.

161

Sometimes the Activist will find the Cheerleader too shallow, or the interests of the two will vary. And their pacing is different. However, they both love people. When they understand each other's strengths and challenges, they are able to form a successful partnership.

Activists typically shy away from *Actors*. They don't understand the Actor's bold behavior, and they think the Actor is always vying to be the center of attention. Many Activists will feel unappreciated or even hurt by the Actor, who is prone to make derogatory or sarcastic remarks about some belief held by the Activist. These two Character Codes avoid one another and do not move in the same business or social circles. Occasionally, some Activists will be enamored with an Actor's persona and follow the person like a groupie. Yet it is almost always an unequal relationship and not a healthy dynamic.

The *Activist* gets along with many *Scholars*—if they aren't too dogmatic. These two move at a similar pace, and both feel strongly about their passion of choice. Conflict arises when the Activist makes a decision based more on feelings and intuition, which the Scholar diminishes by asking for the evidence. With mutual respect, it can be a complementary partnership, the Activist connecting with people and the Scholar handling the data. The Activist avoids the Scholar if the latter behaves in a derisive manner or belittles the Activist's beliefs. This duo leans toward safe, calm, and very tame partnerships. As partners, they are even more dynamic when there is an infusion of energy from another Character Code.

The *Activist* feels most at home in a room filled with other *Activists*. These are their people, deep feeling, passionate about a cause, willing to take the time to converse and really connect. In these relationships there can be a lot of support and safety to express any belief that others may deem unusual. However, there is also an expectation for a certain set of political, business, and ecological beliefs. Two Activists in a partnership will have the greatest chance of success when they partner with or receive advice from a third party that is detail oriented.

The *Activist* gets along well with the *Artist* Character Code. The Activist appreciates the Artist's unique take on life, strong opinions, and support for the underdog. Conflict may arise between these two when each is passionate about opposing causes. When they are on the same page, they make for a strong union or partnership and can be very supportive. Artists can encourage Activists to step out of their comfort zone of community and take a stand as an individual.

The Artist Character Code

The *Artist* is often drawn to the decisive and confident nature of the *Class President*. The Artist admires the way the Class President moves in the world and is able to handle a variety of situations. Conflict arises when the Class President rapid-fires potential solutions to a problem the Artist voices without allowing the Artist an opportunity to come up with a solution. This has the effect of making the Artist feel incompetent, even though the Class President is just offering his or her best help, without realizing the Artist just needs to be heard. Yet this is a powerful union when they both play to their strengths, allowing the Class President to be strategic and the Artist to be creative.

The *Artist* appreciates that the *Cheerleader* likes things aesthetically pleasing, even though their tastes may be quite different. This can be a great combination socially because the Cheerleader moves through crowds and makes connections with ease, whereas the Artist may initially feel somewhat uncomfortable or shy. Once a connection is made, the Artist is freed up to initiate the deeper conversation. These two can be an effective team in working a room. Discord might arise over their differences in handling conflict; the Cheerleader prefers to make light of a situation or dance around it, but the Artist feels the slights and wounds more deeply and may tend to withdraw. A Cheerleader can be great at helping an Artist dispel those feelings.

The *Artist* Character Code is the most tolerant of the *Actor's* grandiose behavior. The Artist understands the Actor's need for significance and often appreciates the Actor's talents. The Artist is not only willing but often desirous of surrendering the spotlight to the Actor. Conflict may arise when the Actor doesn't feed the Artist's own need for significance or give the Artist private recognition, kudos, or respect. When Artists and Actors share mutual respect and make allowances for one another, they are a strong duo. Actors can help bring Artists out of hiding and expose them to new people, fun, and adventure. Even so, their pacing is very different, and the Artist may need to retreat for some recovery time alone.

Creating Better Characters

Contributed by Edith K.

Probably the most fun I've had with Character Coding for work has been using the Codes to develop the characters for a screenplay I've been cowriting! Understanding a character's motivation is important when writing dialogue.

I struggled for a while and then it hit me! I have an entire book about people sitting on my desk—the Character Code System! Character development made easy! Now, when I write the bio of a character, such as an Artist, I have a much clearer image of who they are and how they will behave!

The *Artist* finds the *Scholar's* dry and offbeat humor very amusing. Artists are often confused by the Scholar's driving need for certainty, but once it's explained, they understand where the Scholar is coming from. Artists and Scholars are able to engage in a deep conversation on a topic both find stimulating, but one that would confuse or disinterest others. One such example recently overheard was a conversation between a Scholar and an Artist about bees, the production of honey, and the impact on local produce. Scholars can provide structure and data for an Artist but are unlikely to nurture the Artist's driving need for significance.

Artists have an easy time connecting with most *Activists*. They share some key character traits, their pacing is similar, and they both will take the time to engage in conversation. The Artist appreciates the Activist's need for connection and enjoys hearing about the Activist's beliefs, interests, and passions. Conflict arises if the Activist takes a hard stance in one political corner and the Artist is in another. An Activist can help an Artist be sociable and bridge that initial barrier when connecting with others.

Artists relish the company of other *Artists*. They respect each other's unique point of view and understand the creative process. This may be an "anything goes" relationship with very little room for judgment. In a partnership it can be a great matchup, but it runs into the problem of their having the same strengths and same challenges. It is helpful if each focuses on specific projects and creative elements or if one is more task oriented than the other.

Want a list of the best business or client matchups for you? Download the resource "Shortcut to the Best Character Code Matchups" at http://charactercode.com/matchup.

Combo Character Codes

Can you be more than just one Character Code? That's the question I get asked most often, and the answer is yes, absolutely. You may have some of each Character Code in you; however, there will always be one or a combination of two that will most represent the dominant aspect of your personality.

Any combination is possible. It is the combination of dominant and recessive aspects that makes each of us unique. For example, two women who are related and have Class President–Cheerleader traits are similar but not exactly alike. One has a dominant Class President, while the other has a dominant Cheerleader. And of course, even though they are related, they still have unique life experiences that impact who they are, how they perceive the world, and what they do.

Some combinations are less common, such as a Cheerleader-Scholar. Individuals with this combination often feel like they whiplash between their desire to have it all in order, do it right, and make it fun. The Class President–Activist is also a less frequent blending, with an interesting mix of wanting to take the time to connect and nurture versus feeling the need to get things done.

When determining if people are composed of more than one Character Code, you can assess them by evaluating their driving need and their psyche. Do they demonstrate a clear mix of two Character Code behaviors? You can also see this expressed in their appearance, presentation, and speaking style. For example, is the person in front of you dressed like a Class President but also is wearing flower jewelry, has a wavy hairdo, and smiles a lot? Does she focus intently in a conversation and then get distracted and bounce off to the next person? Does she ask you to "get to the point" but also takes the time to enjoy a good laugh with you? If yes, looks like you just met a Class President–Cheerleader Character Code combo.

That said, typically one Character Code dominates. The quickest way to tell is by determining which driving need is predominantly displayed. Using the example above, if this woman leaned more toward Class President traits, it means that although she values certainty and variety, she cares the most about certainty. So in a business deal or client interaction, make sure you serve the need for certainty first and foremost. But if you also serve her need for variety, you will have a very happy client.

Remember that the four driving needs are things we all want and value—but based on our dominant Character Code, only one driving need will exert the greatest influence in our decision making. That need is very powerful. When you know yours, you can look back over your life and see how often it directed your behavior in work, education, relationships—often without your awareness of its power over you. That need represents your dominant Character Code, and any others are of lesser influence.

Some people want to know exactly what percentage they are of one Character Code or another, and we can test for that. However, I think there is little need to make it complicated. You can see how people show up and what behaviors they express, allowing you to quickly determine if they are more of one Character Code than another. The point isn't to put someone in a box or turn a natural evaluation into a checklist. The ultimate goal is to use the Character Codes as a tool for understanding self and others.

The Four Most Common Character Code Combinations

There are four combinations that are common. You will see them everywhere you go. They are:

» The Class President–Cheerleader
» The Cheerleader-Activist
» The Activist-Scholar
» The Scholar–Class President

The Class President–Cheerleader Combination

The *Class President–Cheerleader* combination is a risk taker. People in this category are decisive, move fast, have a big vision, and can outline the steps it takes to accomplish it. They have a high tolerance for stress, pressure, and pace. They often grow quickly and excel as leaders. You will find many of these combinations in sales, speaking, and executive roles. They often have the ambition and drive to head up large organizations. They need to be mindful of growing too fast, taking on too many tasks or roles, or assuming too much risk. They often struggle with issues of delegation, leverage, and scalability.

The Cheerleader-Activist Combination

The *Cheerleader–Activist* is a people person. Individuals in this category struggle the most with tasks and details. They often have a big vision, many ideas, and dreams to make a difference in the world. They are typically very kind, deep-feeling people motivated by serving and not sales. Their challenges often include managing money, being able to say no, managing time, and finding their own voice. With the combination of a driving need for variety and connection, they often start new activities or meet new people and then bounce off to the next group. This doesn't allow enough time or exposure for an activity or relationship to develop; thus it is difficult for them to create momentum. With support, organization, and focus, they can accomplish great things.

Sister to Sister

Contributed by Mary L.

My sister and I are both Class President–Cheerleader combo Character Codes. We have many of the same traits, but my dominant Class President and her dominant Cheerleader definitely set us apart.

If I am in a hurry, I want people to just get to the point when they are telling a story. When I used to write e-mails, I was very direct in my message.

One day, my sister looked over an e-mail I had sent and gently told me that my e-mail sounded curt. I reread it, and it did sound curt, although I was just getting to the point. From then on, I had my sister read my drafts and put the "nicey-nice" words in there to soften up my tone.

We also used to go to a lot of networking events together. My Cheerleader–Class President sister was a natural at meeting new people. I tend to be the quiet one.

When we met people, I noticed my sister liked to talk a lot during these conversations. It was hard for anyone else to get a word in edgewise with her, including me!

When someone else did have a chance to speak, she would blurt out or interrupt with something else she had just thought of. It was frustrating for me, and she had no idea she was doing this.

After learning Character Coding, I was able to gently share my observation. Since then, she has become aware about talking too much and now listens more often.

The Activist-Scholar Combination

The *Activist-Scholar* combination can often be described as the "absent-minded professor." An easy way to tell whether this combination leans more toward Activist or Scholar is to look at the person's hair. If the person is a man and his hair tends to be neat with a shorter cut, then he has more Scholar. If his hair tends to look more windblown, unruly, or overgrown, then he has more Activist. This also tells you whether the driving need for connection or certainty is most important to him. Activist-Scholars often want to engage with people and connect over topics they find of interest, and they may converse at length. They tend to be less aware of social graces and sometimes present as awkward or clumsy. When angry, this combination can tend toward being passive-aggressive or holding grudges.

The Class President–Scholar Combination

The *Class President–Scholar* is not a people person. In this combo Code, people are very task oriented, have a strong driving need for certainty, and want things done the "right" way. They are often removed emotionally and prefer empirical data over experiential perceptions. They are likely to say, "Where is the evidence?" They are often minimalists, can be rigid in their body stance, and show up wearing tailored clothing with clean lines in neutral or dark colors and feel safest when the rules are followed. They can be very exacting and literal.

A combo Code can express any of the characteristics listed from either of its two Character Codes. I remember a client saying, "I think I only express the negative traits of both of my Character Codes." We had a laugh about that, and I reassured her that no one is locked into a certain set of positive or negative traits. We are human, and our expressed behavior evolves depending on many factors, such as our current life situation, work environment, and other circumstances. We can always improve our attitude, work on our challenges, and continue to stretch our personal and professional limitations. Access the "Character Codes Combos" chart in color at http://charactercode.com/combos.

Exacting Nature

In a previous career, I worked on many projects with a Scholar–Class President Character Code. We had many things in common, but sometimes his exacting nature would rub me the wrong way.

On one such day I was rushing to get to an event we were both attending for work that began at 9 a.m. Now, many planners were involved in this event, and so it wasn't essential that I be there from setup to strike. I did, however, need to arrive before the presentations began, as I was introducing our speaker.

So I texted my colleague and friend to confirm what time the event would start, as he knew I needed to provide that introduction. He replied, telling me it was 8 a.m.

Now I was in a panic, as I thought it started at 9 a.m. I had to move even faster to get there on time and arrived feeling more than a little frazzled.

Once there I just saw attendees milling about the room, enjoying the continental breakfast and chatting. The doors opened at 8 a.m. for networking, and the presentations began at 9 a.m.

I complained to my colleague about his text response. He held his ground, stating he had answered the question correctly and wasn't interested in seeing my point of view.

After all, the event *did* start at 8 a.m.!

Marketing to Combo Character Codes

The four combinations above are common enough that you could select one of them as your ideal client profile. I would not recommend marketing to another Character Code combination because either the pool of candidates isn't large enough or it would dilute or confuse your marketing message. The four combinations represented are so pervasive in our society that they will recognize themselves in your client attraction efforts and come knocking at your door. I have built different aspects of my business using the combination Character Code profiles and have seen the results every time. Chapter 10 focuses on how to begin marketing to single or combo Character Codes.

It pays to be aware of the relationships described in this chapter. The Character Codes with whom you choose to work or play will impact much of your waking hours. Choose them wisely. Don't let them drive you crazy. Take a turn looking at life from their perspective.

Character Codes and Culture

Different countries can have a dominant Character Code culture. Of course, every Character Code will be present, but the prevailing personality of the community will impact the beliefs and attitudes of a specific country or area.

Many describe Germany as a Class President Character Code culture. People in Germany value efficiency, which has been demonstrated in the best and worst of ways throughout history.

England can be described as having a Scholar Character Code culture with a strong belief in education, with many English families raising their children to go to Oxford.

Many Asian cultures also value a Class President or Scholar mindset, which can be challenging if you are a Cheerleader or Activist born in that environment.

Certain communities and geographical areas have an Activist vibe, such as Byron Bay, Australia, or Santa Cruz, California.

Some northeastern regions of the United States have a decidedly Scholar attitude, and Seattle, Washington, has an Artist feel.

Many would describe France, Italy, and Brazil as nations of Actors, and you'll find many Cheerleaders in the southern United States.

How to Read a Client Now

Now that you know how the Character Codes get along and have been introduced to combo Character Coding, remember to:

» Notice the people you enjoy spending the most time with at work and determine which Character Codes they are.

» Think of your friends and family in your personal life, noting if you see a pattern in their character.

» List which Character Codes you naturally connect with and which ones you find a real challenge.

» Identify the personality traits you could work on to be a better communicator and connector with other Character Codes.

» Become aware of the differences and sometimes subtle distinctions that set apart a singular from a combo Character Code.

Chapter 10 will introduce the use of Character Coding in marketing and sales, provide tips to quickly identify your ideal Character Code client, describe turn-ons and turnoffs for client attraction, and outline best practices for working a room.

Take the following action steps now:

» Download the resource "Shortcut to the Best Character Code Matchups" at http://charactercode.com/matchup.

» Access the "Character Codes Combos" chart in color at http://charactercode.com/combos.

TEN

The Character Codes in Marketing and Sales

How to Attract Your Ideal Client

O NCE YOU'VE LEARNED the Character Code System, it becomes all about its application. How do you use it in everyday life?

Marketing and Selling with the Character Codes

My readers interested in marketing and sales will want to remember how to select ideal clients based on their Character Code and how to serve their driving need. Here are some ideas intended to get you started. Remember these key points when marketing and selling to the Character Codes:

Serving the Driving Needs

The *Class President's* driving need is certainty. Make sure you focus on the specific results and do what you say you'll do. Make sure to convey confidence and get to the point. The Class President's main issue is *trust*. Gain it and you have satisfied his or her need for certainty.

The *Cheerleader's* driving need is variety. Make sure you focus on the fun and the newness and assure Cheerleaders that life won't be boring. Then reassure them that they won't be going it alone. The main issue for the Cheerleader is feeling *alive*.

The *Actor's* driving need is significance with a spotlight. Make sure you focus on Actors by giving them lots of attention and by demonstrating that you see their value and talent. They have big energy and are often misunderstood. The main issue for the Actor is being *seen*.

The *Scholar's* driving need is certainty. Make sure you focus on the facts and provide data, details, and specifics. Allow Scholars time to decide and do research. The main issue for the Scholar is *trust*.

The *Activist's* driving need is connection. Make sure you focus on the personal connection, displaying your humanity and caring. Let Activists know you will be supportive throughout the journey. The main issue for the Activist is feeling *loved*.

The *Artist's* driving need is significance without the spotlight. Make sure you focus on the Artist as an individual. Acknowledge that Artists are different and unique and are not interested in a cookie-cutter solution. They care about self-expression and creativity. The main issue for the Artist is being *seen*.

Make yourself necessary to somebody.
—Ralph Waldo Emerson, American poet and essayist

Marketing to the Character Codes Online

The *Class President* is attracted to websites that have an overall corporate, clean, or minimal look that conveys the message of confidence, trust, and success. Avoid earthy, pastel, or floral colors and excessive prints or patterns; instead stick with blues, black, grays, browns, white, or other neutrals. In your marketing language and copy, be sure to quickly get to the point and be results driven.

The *Cheerleader* loves browsing stylish, upbeat websites that convey a message of fun and high energy. Avoid looking too corporate, as Cheerleaders equate that with being boring. Stick with bright, vibrant, or romantic colors and do not use an earthy or neutral palette. Your marketing language should express excitement and be very personable.

The *Actor* is drawn to a website that is stylish and hip, looks polished, and conveys a message of success, competence, and savvy. Color choices can range from classic to romantic to loud with "flashing lights" as long as you avoid anything too earthy, neutral, or "woo-woo." In your copy, focus on big results and high energy, and you can push the envelope with your language.

The *Scholar* prefers a functional, easy-to-navigate website with a corporate and conservative look. The message to convey is one of competence, noting your use of systems and data. Avoid flowery colors, patterns, or anything that sends the message of drama, sticking with a tried-and-true neutral and solid-color palette. Your marketing language will be most effective if it is factual, detached, and objective.

The *Activist* feels most connected with a website that is engaging and personable. Your overall look can range from calming to upbeat. Colors can run the gamut from earthy to vibrant; just avoid black, neon, or any combination that doesn't look harmonious. Your marketing language should be very personal, focus on the connection, go deep, and stay grounded. New age or friendly copy is preferred over business lingo.

The *Artist* is turned off by a corporate, busy, or template-style website. Artists are attracted to sites that look original, stylish, eclectic, and hip and are custom built. The message should express individuality and passion for your cause, product, or service. You can use any type of color palette or combination, and the more creative the better. Your marketing language should speak in your unique voice and represent your distinct opinions.

The only important thing about design is how it relates to people.

—Victor Papanek, designer and educator

How the Character Codes Buy

The *Class President* will make a quick decision and gives a very definitive answer. Class Presidents are unlikely to change their minds once they commit. They will question you about your process just long enough to be assured that you know what you are doing, and they do not actually want to know all the details of the *how* behind your service or product. Class Presidents are very results oriented and like things to be done quickly.

The *Cheerleader* also makes a quick buying decision motivated by feelings and emotions. This is the Character Code most likely to make impulsive or last-minute purchases. Cheerleaders don't like the buying process to be tedious, involve too many steps, or take too long. They are bored with the details involving your process or your instructions for a product and are motivated by the end result or promised transformation. They often place higher value on their intuition or the buying experience over the actual product.

The *Actor* also arrives at a quick yes or no, and it is often a no. It is tough to grab an Actor's attention and even more challenging to earn an Actor's respect. Actors want big results in the shortest amount of time and will be very distrusting of you and your product. They will question your process and attempts to rewrite your rules. They can also become overwhelmed or not follow through if your selling process involves multiple steps or an extended length of time.

The *Scholar* likes to crunch the data and arrive at a logical conclusion. Scholars do not want to feel rushed, and so if there is a time limit in your buying process, it will need to be driven by a legitimate reason or they will not trust you. They like follow-up details and information about your process and are turned off by any presentation that seems "salesy" or hyped. They want to make an unemotional buying decision driven by their head and not their heart.

The *Activist* is always looking to have more time when it comes to making a purchase. Activists are naturally cautious and want to make a careful decision. They are slower to buy, and their yes response comes from their intuition and a heart-based or "gut" feeling. They also are influenced by group consensus or their community's opinion. The buying process is easier when there is an element of support to guide them through the execution of your service or product.

The *Artist* is also a cautious buyer that carefully considers making a purchase. Artists are looking for a personal connection and want to know that you "get them" via either your service or product. Ideally, they would prefer individual attention and customized service and are turned off by the "one-size-fits-all" approach. They are not looking for templates. When their driving need is met, they can become very loyal and long-term customers.

Dialed in to What Clients Need

Contributed by Gurpreet K.

I am a portrait photographer and have applied Character Coding in my business. Previously, I had a client who said I gave him too much information regarding the preparation for a session, which made me think maybe I should edit it down a bit. I realize now that this client was just a Cheerleader, and I now tailor my sales presentation for who is in front of me.

From the time I answer calls or e-mail clients, I work with them according to their needs. I figure out their Character Code by the way they speak on the phone or the way they have written their e-mail. I accordingly send them the information that they would need to make their decision.

One of my clients was a Scholar, and I provided information about how to prep, including the clothing, the time of the session, the location, etc. We had a conversation about places where she could hang her artwork even before the portrait session was done. She loved working with me and all the details I provided.

I have an Actress client who also raves about me, because I was able to make the session spontaneous and fun, all about her and her family.

I have always loved my profession, but Character Coding makes it fun to work with all different individuals!

I never recommend selecting an ideal Character Code client based on buying patterns. Instead, select your ideal client based on who you are, what your message is, and whom you want to work with; you can always adjust your business practices, marketing, and sales to accommodate your ideal client.

Certainly there are things in life that money can't buy, but it's very funny—Did you ever try buying them without money?

—Ogden Nash, American writer and humorist

Focused Marketing Message

Marketing is about getting your message out there whether you are a big business, entrepreneur, service provider, or small mom-and-pop store. The greatest success I see is when you have a clearly identified persona behind your business that is designed to communicate with and attract a specific ideal client. When you are an entrepreneur, that person is you and why you do what you do. When you are a major corporation, it is the brand identity you build.

When you try to market to everyone, you invariably market to no one.

—Anonymous

Once you are clear about your identity in business, you will need to decide whom you want to attract as potential clients. Some use target marketing, niche marketing, or demographics to accomplish this. Many businesses allot extensive budgets for marketing research and focus groups. My bias is for using the Character Codes instead of traditional demographics, especially for businesses that engage in affinity marketing practices. Knowing your ideal client's driving need, fears, dreams, personal branding style, and emotional triggers is invaluable when it comes to creating a highly responsive marketing campaign.

So which Character Code should you select? Any of the six is fine as long as it is in alignment with your business and what you offer. You could even run campaigns that market your product to different Character Codes and test the response. While a short test is fine, you don't want to try to market to every Character Code on an ongoing basis. It would be cost prohibitive to run ongoing simultaneous campaigns, and if you try to reach everyone, it will dilute your marketing message.

Here is an example of when it doesn't work. *John is a fitness trainer and owns a small, local gym. His business is thriving, and he decides he wants to break into the online market. His ideal Character Code clients are Cheerleader women who love attending his exercise boot camp and enjoy the social atmosphere he provides. It doesn't hurt that he is very "easy on the eyes," funny, and motivating as he leads his workouts. John hires a company to turn his routine into a virtual product. The graphic design is bold and masculine looking, John isn't shown in the marketing, the social component of the workout has been removed, and very few sales of the product are generated.* The product was not in alignment with the business persona or the ideal client.

Here is an example of when it does work. *Stacey also has a successful small gym serving Cheerleaders as her ideal Character Code client. She, too, wants to break into the online market. Stacey knows that her Cheerleader clients love coming to see her in person. Over the years she has consulted with many Class President women that say they want to get in shape but don't have the time to drive to her gym and spend an hour exercising. Stacey decides to create a virtual workout that can be done in only 15 minutes for 4 days each week. She markets it to Class Presidents, appealing to their desire to get exercise "done" and checked off their list, without wasting any time. She focuses on the efficiency and is specific about the results they can expect with certainty. The product is selling well online.* This product was designed to meet the driving need of the client.

Marketing to Two Character Codes

You may be asking, "What if I want to market to two Character Code clients at one time?" It is easier and more impactful if you just focus on one. You will get more bang for your marketing buck with one ideal

Character Code client and a clear, consistent message. If you do want to market to a broader audience, then stick with one of the combo Character Codes listed below. These four combos are prevalent enough in our society that you will generate a significant response.

» The Class President–Cheerleader
» The Cheerleader-Activist
» The Activist-Scholar
» The Scholar–Class President

Here's an example of how to market to a Character Code combo using the Activist-Scholar. You would want to focus on the traits described in Chapter 8 and then also bring in the characteristics described in each individual Character Code chapter—particularly the traits or trends the Character Codes have in common. When you effectively apply this strategy to your marketing, your message will be consistent. The majority of the client base would be Activist-Scholar along with some solo Activist or Scholar Character Codes responding to your promotion. You would want to avoid marketing to other combos, such as the Cheerleader-Scholar. Although they do exist, it would have a whiplash effect to combine those traits in your promotional efforts and dilute your marketing.

> *It doesn't matter which side of the fence you get off on sometimes. What matters most is getting off. You cannot make progress without making decisions.*
>
> **—Jim Rohn, author, speaker**

Using the Character Codes in Any Market

The advantage of using Character Coding in your marketing and sales is not only to target your ideal clients but to have them feel understood and seen. So what does this mean if your product or service isn't about making money, building a business, or solving any other revenue problem? Can you use the Character Codes in a soft skills market? Absolutely.

Here's a quick overview to get you started in thinking about how to apply Character Coding to a soft skills market such as relationships and dating.

Class Presidents are easy to identify on a first date. During the conversation, you may hear them speak this way: "I like A and B but can't stand C." Their ideal date is a planned adventure with a known outcome. The secret fear that keeps them from a relationship is the fear of becoming dependent on their partner. To compensate, they often choose to remain alone. If they are in a relationship and it doesn't work out, they will ultimately blame themselves for making a poor choice and being vulnerable, no matter what role the other person played in the breakup.

I'll Have What You Are Having . . .

In the movie *Runaway Bride*, Julia Roberts played the role of a Cheerleader Character Code. She would date, become engaged, and almost marry one suitor after another, only to flee at the last minute. Each time she dated a suitor, she would say she liked her eggs cooked the same as his.

When she had some time on her own, she worked to really discover who she was and what she liked. There is a great scene where she tries every type of egg: scrambled, poached, over easy, hard boiled.

What did she discover? That she didn't like eggs.

This is a great snapshot of a Cheerleader woman, wanting to be liked and always worrying about pleasing others. Cheerleaders often decide how they feel based on the feedback they get from the outside world. Many Cheerleader women make this journey of self-discovery at some point in their lives, where they turn inward to learn what it is they really like and learn more about who they are.

Cheerleaders are quickly spotted on a first date, too. During their conversation, they are likely to say something akin to "I like whatever you like." Their ideal date would be an amusement park adventure, shopping, or dancing. The secret fear keeping them from a relationship is being alone or rejected. To compensate, they will often date constantly, moving from relationship to relationship, always the one to end it. If they are in a relationship and it doesn't work out, they will ultimately blame their partner because they don't wish to look inward.

Actors are also easily identifiable on a first date. During conversation, you may hear them say something like, "I like capital A with cowboy boots and a tiara." Their ideal date is being driven in a Bentley to a five-star dinner or a private poolside cabana. The secret fear preventing them from developing a romantic relationship is that they are not lovable on the inside. To compensate, they will often appear shallow or uninterested or will always be performing. If they are in a relationship and it doesn't work out, they will blame their partner on the outside while really blaming themselves internally.

Scholars on a first date would be tough to miss. During the conversation you may hear, "I don't like it, and here are the three reasons why . . ." Their ideal date is a museum visit, a classical music performance, or a nice dinner. The secret fear that keeps Scholars from a relationship is concern that their partner will keep them from their intellectual pursuits. To compensate, they often compartmentalize themselves in the relationship. If they are in a relationship and it doesn't work out, they will ultimately blame their partner for taking them away from what mattered to them.

Men and women belong to different species and communications between them is still in its infancy.

—Bill Cosby, comedian

Activists on a first date may say, "I like what is best for all of us." Their ideal date is taking a walk in nature, having a picnic, or sitting under a tree and watching the sunset. The secret fear that keeps them from a relationship is that they think they aren't worthy. To compensate, they often focus on taking care of others. If they are in a relationship and it doesn't work out, they will ultimately blame themselves because they believe they are lacking.

And as with the other Character Codes, *Artists* are also quite recognizable on a first date. During the conversation, you may hear them say, "You wouldn't understand what I like." Their ideal date would be attending a concert, taking a stroll in an art gallery, or engaging in an activity off the beaten path. The secret fear that keeps them from a relationship is losing their sense of self. To compensate, they often set boundaries and keep their distance. If they are in a relationship and it doesn't work out, they will ultimately blame society for trying to make them conform.

It doesn't matter what your business model is or which niche your product serves, you can use Character Coding to market and sell to your potential clients.

Face-to-Face with the Character Codes

At this point in the book, you are likely an expert in Character Coding. However, a few additional tips for how to quickly spot your ideal client from across the room will benefit you.

Tips to Quickly Identify the Character Codes in Person

You'll notice that this chart has three columns, respectively labeled "Task," "People," and "Both." When you are deciding between one Character Code and another, it often comes down to the two choices in a column, either the Character Code on the top or the one on the bottom—I refer to this as Character Code pairing. You may access the chart in color at http://charactercode.com/thinkfast.

What you will also notice is that the Class President, Cheerleader, and Actor are in the top row and identified as "faster," while the Scholar, Activist, and Artist are in the bottom row and identified as "slower." This refers to the way the Character Codes process and assimilate information. It also translates into the way they move, speak, and observe the world around them.

Whether or not it is better to be faster or slower depends entirely on the individual who is rendering the opinion. There are an equal number of situations where moving fast or slow can be a plus or minus. This difference in speed is one of the easiest ways to distinguish someone from across the room, aside from the obvious appearance choices and personal branding.

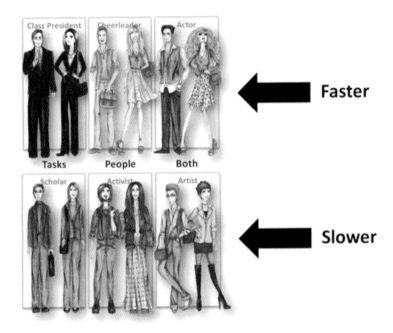

Character Code Pairing

In the chart, the Class President is stacked on top of the Scholar, as both are task oriented. While they may sometimes appear similar, speed is one of the great divides between the two. You will notice this difference in pacing in body movement, speaking style, and decision making. A *Class President* will watch the room with intensity, move decisively, and attempt to control or act as a leader in a problem-solving situation. The *Scholar* is more likely to observe the room from the sidelines, move with deliberation, and complain or comment on what is not working in a problematic situation.

Character Code Coaching

Contributed by Mary L.

One of the best things about Character Coding for my business is knowing who my ideal clients are. It's not to say I wouldn't work with the other Character Codes, but I prefer certain some over others.

I am a Class President–Cheerleader, and I like working with clients that are like me. Why? Because I notice when I advise Class Presidents, they get it done right away. But I also like it if they have some Cheerleader traits in them, because we tend to laugh together and be more relaxed.

In working with clients, I've seen the Cheerleaders talk a lot, and they move from one task to another without finishing any of them. They also get sidetracked easily with the "shiny penny" opportunities that surround them.

The Actors often want to do everything over the top but then get overwhelmed when it actually comes down to doing it.

The Artists spend the most time with the aesthetics and look of their websites and marketing materials to make sure everything shows their uniqueness.

The Activists get stuck in the cycle of not knowing if they should be following their heart or their head in making business decisions.

And the Scholars tend to ask a lot of questions and want to know all the details and the outcome before taking the steps to get started. But once they get started, they get it done perfectly.

Knowing who my ideal clients are makes it so much easier to create effective marketing materials to promote my business.

The middle column shows the Cheerleader stacked on the Activist, as both are people oriented. Again, a major difference is the speed at which they operate. A *Cheerleader* will move quickly around the room, socially engage with a number of people, and radiate a bubbly, extroverted energy. An *Activist* is more likely to stay in one area of the room, make deeper connections with single individuals, and project a calm, introverted energy.

The last column shows the Actor stacked on top of the Artist, and they both can switch between being people oriented and task oriented. The major divide between the two is their speed and desire for the spotlight (the Actor) or dislike for the spotlight (the Artist). An *Actor* emanates a powerful and commanding energy in the room, prefers to be the center of attention, and often overlooks the people around him or her. An *Artist* has the ability to sneak into a room unnoticed, likes to remain along the fringe, and observes everyone else in the room, particularly noting those that others are ignoring.

Understanding this chart and the major distinctions drawn in each of the Character Code chapters will have you reading people from across the room in no time!

Personality has the power to open many doors, but character must keep them open.

—Anonymous

Client Attraction Turnoffs and Turn-ons

There are some universal practices that serve as a client attractor (or detractor) with all people. It is wise to understand these distinctions in your marketing and to realize that certain Character Codes may be more influenced by some practices than other Character Codes. Review the list below for common client attraction turnoffs and turn-ons.

Client Detraction—the Turnoffs

>> You confuse marketing with sales.

» You are always pushing.

» You always meet your needs first.

» You are always a walking advertisement.

» You don't have active listening skills.

» You don't represent who you are behind the business.

Client Attraction—the Turn-ons

» You are dedicated to providing value.

» You have a sense of humor.

» You are real.

» You are personable, but you don't air your dirty laundry.

» You respect your audience's autonomy and intelligence.

» You give first.

» You interact and engage online.

» You have a clear message.

» You have a process that guides people from A to B.

» You are open for business (people know how to find you).

» You know what your client needs.

These client detraction–attraction methods are noticeable in print, online, via phone, and by other marketing means. They are the most noticeable in person, which is where you will see the quickest yes or no response. After reading the chapters covering first impressions, you know that the opportunity to impact a potential client through networking can come and go in a flash. Knowing the best practices for working a room can make or break your client attraction strategy.

The richest people in the world look for and build networks,
everyone else looks for work.

—Robert Kiyosaki, entrepreneur, author

Best Practices for How to Work a Room—Top 10 Tips

The ability to connect with people in person will never go out of style. Perhaps you are an entrepreneur frequenting the local networking gatherings, a sales director pitching to businesses each week, or an executive meeting with potential investors; any way you look at it, you need to know how to work a room. Even the phenomenon of social media and online marketing will not eliminate the power of the person-to-person connection; it will only make it stronger, more exclusive, and therefore more highly coveted.

In an infamous *New York Times* survey on social anxiety, the thought of walking into a room filled with strangers and the idea of then speaking were listed as the top two fears. Death was number three.[1]

What does this mean for you? That there is a good chance that this fear is holding you back in your business networking and an even stronger likelihood that you will encounter someone in the room who is feeling this fear.

This means that to successfully work a room, your number one job is to connect with people in a way that makes both of you feel comfortable. Here are my tried-and-true "Top 10 Tips for Working a Room" that every Character Code can immediately put to use.

1. **Be ready for the opportunity.** Have very short responses to sum up who you are, what you do, what you offer, what you are working on, and what kind of people you are looking to connect with. What is most important is to not deliver all this information at one time or in a monologue or to have it sound canned.

2. **Know what you want.** Why are you going to the event? Are you looking for a client? Are you trying to sell a product, find an investor, build a network, look for a joint venture partner? Think long term and determine how the people you meet today could develop into strong business relationships in the future.

A Covert Cheerleader in Action

Contributed by Jenny C.

Due to the added benefit of Character Coding, making connections is even easier. Now I feel like a covert agent with secret intelligence when interacting with people at networking events.

When in a conversation, I can adapt my language and mannerisms to better connect with that person in order to have a deeper, more meaningful conversation and outcome.

One time I almost forgot this valuable lesson while networking, and a prospective Activist client visibly started backing away from me. My zealous Cheerleader energy was a bit overwhelming for her.

I was able to save the situation by backing off and then referred her to an Activist colleague that would match her energy and really "get" her.

As a result, the woman was very grateful for the introduction, and my colleague loved receiving the referral.

A "covert Cheerleader" saved the networking day!

Networking isn't selling; there's a strong perception that you go to networking events to sell as hard as you can and find clients. That's not how it works. Occasionally you might meet someone who later becomes a customer, but the majority are there to sell themselves—so I can't think of a worse place to try and sell because no one's there to buy.

—Andy Lopata, author, speaker, and former managing director of the Business Referral Exchange

3. **Make a great first impression.** Know who you are and what message you want to send. Know what type of event

you are going to and what the likely mix in the room will be. Create your personal branding so you feel empowered and influence people's assumptions you wish to impact.

4. **Know your people.** Use Character Coding to quickly read the room and decide whom to approach and connect with. Look, listen, and learn who the people are so you can communicate in a way that ensures that your message lands with them. Remember the driving needs and see how you can serve your potential clients' driving needs in that first interaction.

5. **Observe and move.** Don't rush into the event so fast that you are a whirlwind, leaping without looking. Don't delay so long that you miss opportunities and hug the wall. Observe the group, see which people you want to connect with, and make your move. Tailor your entrance into a conversation based on the people you see in front of you. A good rule of thumb is a friendly smile and disarming greeting that introduces you into the conversation.

6. **Engage in a conversation.** If you only think about what you want to say and don't listen to what the other person is saying, then it is merely people talking at each other; they're just polite enough to take turns. A true conversation is unique to each individual because it is influenced by what the other person says—your input and the other person's response. That is a dialogue.

7. **Listen and give first.** Listening is your best skill in a networking situation. It will allow you the opportunity to hear what the person needs, wants, and desires. Be ready and willing to provide a resource, advice, or solution if requested (or ask first if the person is looking for feedback). Act as the "host" and see whom you can connect others with at the same event. Be the hub or connector in the room. Be generous.

8. **Vary the staging.** You may want to be in the middle of the group and at the center of attention, or you may want to be along the fringe connecting with those on the outskirts of the

room. There is opportunity in both places, and it pays to vary your movement. Sometimes the best connections happen in the hallway, before the event starts and, often, long after the event ends. Vary your approach, timing, position. Try something different and note the results.

9. **Power-network like a pro.** Want to double your connections and accelerate your results? Bring a buddy. Ideally, a business partner or colleague. This way you can both work separate parts of the room and make introductions for one another. This type of cross-promoting utilizes a third-party testimonial right when you are in the room along with an immediate in-person introduction—that's powerful! If you don't have a partner, you can do this with a business friend as long as you both understand how to promote one another's work and have a trusting and giving relationship.

If you want to go quickly, go alone. If you want to go far, go together.

—African proverb

10. **Follow up and deepen the connection.** Some people you meet have a steel-trap mind and will remember you forever; more often, however, people are busy, feel overwhelmed, and focus on what is "top of mind." So don't be a hound that chases them down, but do follow up. Find creative ways to reach out and further the connection. Remember, you are building a relationship and not scoring a home run.

Will you automatically conquer your fears as you begin to network? No, but it is a step in the right direction. Networking with a colleague and putting these tips into action will make it easier with repetition—which is what generates the results. Character Coding is invaluable on this path, so get out there and make those connections!

You can't file a conversation.

—Anonymous

How to Read a Client Now

Now that you are learning a new approach to attracting clients, remember to:

» Translate your Character Coding knowledge into your marketing and sales systems. Market and serve the client's driving need.

» Decide which Character Code you are going to select as an ideal client, or are you going to market to one of the four combo Codes?

» Practice making the judgment call quickly using Character Code pairing. Mentally note your decision and then continue observing to see if you got it right. Continue practicing and watch how your communication improves!

» Avoid the client detractors and get your client attractor strategies into place. Notice what might be missing from your business model and implement it so your clients feel heard.

» Get out and be seen. Put the "Top 10 Tips for Working a Room" into action using the Character Codes.

Chapter 11 wraps up the Character Codes so you can start putting what you have learned into action. Additional resources and business advice follow in the Appendix including 11 Pillars for building your business platform and VIP tickets to Client Success LIVE.

Take the following action steps now:

» Access the "Think Fast—Shortcut to Character Coding" pairing chart and resource guide at http://charactercode .com/thinkfast.

» Download the expanded resource "Client Attraction Turnoff's and Turn-on's" at http://charactercode.com/ clientattraction.

» Access the "How to Work a Room" resource and stories to learn more about using Character Coding in your networking at http://charactercode.com/workaroom.

ELEVEN

Putting the Character Codes in Action

Are You Ready to Roll?

BELIEVE THAT ONCE you implement what you have learned, knowledge becomes power. Until then, it is just filler for your head. Action is often the missing ingredient that makes the difference between a life half lived and the life of your dreams.

I realize that each of us is in a different situation. You might be a corporate executive in a fast-paced world of deadlines and ever-increasing demands. Perhaps you are an entrepreneur striving to build a business that thrives in the marketplace. You may be reading this for fun, or perhaps because you want to learn how to get over being shy or how to network and attract more clients. Or you might just want to understand why people do the things they do.

What we all have in common is membership in a club known as the "Human Condition." In this club, our natural brain biology guides us to be comfortable and stay safe. This means that any time we make a change, any time we step out of our comfort zone and take a risk, we are going against our natural biology.

I consider such steps as acts of courage. The size of that first step is different for each one of us. Your first big step may be delivering a five-minute speech in front of an audience. Or it may be gathering your courage to start a multimillion-dollar company.

It is all relative.

What I know to be true is that it's a stretch and an opportunity for growth every step of the way, no matter what type of person you are.

And the most important thing isn't the destination as much as it is the journey. But, yes, the destination can be very motivating too!

I find that individuals on this journey are alert, aware, always learning, and always willing to grow. I consider them extraordinary (and ordinary) people from everyday life who have chosen to embark on a heroic journey. I believe that we all have been given an invitation to show up as the hero in our own lives. Some choose to decline this offer, but there are others brave enough to accept. I consider you in this group!

Now that you have learned the Character Code System, I encourage you to use it as a guide that grants you permission to be who you are. Use it to recognize your strengths and talents and to really soar and create the life you truly desire.

Use the "Psyche" section to get yourself out of the box. Stop limiting your potential and put an end to the cycle of destructive self-talk. Beating yourself up about the things you don't do well is counterproductive. I always view the challenges as an opportunity to invite others in for support, outsource the need, or extend the timeline to complete the challenge.

Taking the Heroic Journey

What's possible when you embark on your own heroic journey? Just about anything you can imagine you can achieve. You can create the business you've always wanted, rise through the corporate ranks, attract endless clients who want what you have to offer, become a philanthropic force in your community, find the love of your life— make it your goal and it is within reach.

I know what it's like to feel discouraged, where that first tiny step seems like it is a mile long. You read about my struggles in the Introduction. It wasn't an easy road; however, I'm infinitely grateful that I traveled that path.

Here are the steps I took on my own heroic journey; feel free to use them as you make your journey:

Reclaim Your Value

If you've been beaten down by a business failure, a series of unhappy clients, a health crisis, or a failed personal relationship, you may feel like you have lost your way. Go back and reread the chapter for your Character Code. Pay attention to your strengths, your gifts, and your talents. Reclaim your value. Remember exactly who you are. Ask yourself, "Why not me?" Instead of making a case for why you cannot do it, ask, "Who am I not to succeed?"

Keep an Open Mind

People who are feeling stuck can make a really good case for it and list all the reasons why they're in the situation. It turns out that many of those reasons have nothing to do with them. I remember a point in my struggles when I thought things would never turn around. No matter what idea others suggested, I could shoot it down. Then I had an epiphany: what was I fighting for? The energy I put into arguing why it wouldn't work could be spent discovering a way to make it work, but that required an open mind. If you are running into your own resistance at every turn, read the inner meanie in the "Psyche" section of your Character Code chapter. Is your resistance valid and something to be mindful of, or is it just an old familiar story you use to hold yourself back?

Invest in Yourself

Many people see the value of spending money on a college education, but they do not understand the need for continuing their education in business. The truth is, every person who was a great success spent time and money investing in professional and personal growth. There are new skills and techniques to learn, training to take, communities of practice to join, networking to do—you name it—the opportunities to better yourself are everywhere, and those people making the effort see the results. I remember when this was a real challenge for me. I wasn't even making it financially, but I knew that without getting the training I needed, I would never have the tools to create the business I wanted. It was a leap of faith for me, just as it is for anyone who says, "Yes, I'm worth investing in myself."

Don't Wait to Be Ready

Some people will get their training and then never get started. Why does that happen? For a variety of reasons, including self-doubt, fear, and one of the most common: thinking they aren't ready. Waiting to be ready is really an excuse, because you are never ready. Even with the best preparation and training, the unexpected can and will occur. You cannot plan for everything, and a huge part of your learning curve happens in the moment—being in the swift-moving river of action. There is no greater teacher than the real thing—to actually go for it and learn from experience.

Lead with Your Heart

Forget bravado. Forget being cool. Forget hiding. Forget being perfect. One of the things that will make you shine in your heroic journey is being true to who you are: brave, vulnerable, real, human, alive. People love the real you. The old system of faceless professionalism for the sake of client customer care is over. Consumers buy based on emotion, and they love connecting with someone or something that has a life and breath behind it. If you represent a big company or product, they want to know what you stand for. If you are a small-business person or service provider, they want to know that you care. Lead with your heart, boldly state what you desire to create, and watch as others get behind you and support you. That comes from being real and sharing your heart.

Be Fully Committed

If you want to make a change, you need to be fully committed and do whatever it takes. When I find people bailing out too soon, it is typically because they got scared and talked themselves into believing whatever they'd gotten into wasn't for them; maybe they thought they weren't good enough or didn't deserve it. Of course, that is just the inner meanie talking. It is never the voice of truth. The other thing I see happen is that people don't pick what they really want. They pick something on the shelf below their dream, so that when they fail, it doesn't really matter—and of course, it always produces exactly that result. They were set up to fail from the start by putting the emphasis on a back-door escape. Why? It wasn't what they really wanted to do anyway. Get yourself fully committed and just go for the big dream, whatever it is. What is the success you really crave?

Do the Work

There is work involved. I don't know of any legal activity to build a successful business and life that didn't involve actual work. It doesn't mean it has to be hard, but it does take consistent effort. Even the overnight success stories tell you there were years of learning and often failures along the journey until people got it right. If you are struggling because of the work investment necessary to create your business, then go back to the Character Codes and refocus on your strengths. Set up your office environment so you are the most productive and get the most support. Most business ventures boil down to a need to attract more clients or generate more sales. Use the Character Codes to make sure you are reaching the best possible clients and speaking to them in their language. Use your Character Coding as your marketing and sales guide.

Continue Developing Your Process

This isn't a one-trick dog-and-pony show. If you want to stay current and relevant for your clients, then you must continue learning and improving your methods. Maybe you make your service faster or more cost effective. Maybe you improve the benefits. Maybe you make adjustments based on changes in the current economic climate or the changing needs of your client base. Whatever the reason, you must constantly refine and develop your process so that you are always current with (or ahead of) the marketplace.

Stretch Your Comfort Zone

I experienced rapid growth and success because I was willing to take risks and get uncomfortable. It became my new norm. Comfortable feels great in the moment, but if you spend a lifetime always trying to maintain this state, it becomes a fairly tame existence. It would also make you very inflexible around other people and in new situations. Learning to step outside your comfort zone is the starting point for creating something new and potentially brilliant. It definitely won't be boring!

Expand Your Vision

What seems like a big, scary goal now will appear easy as you stack up your successes. Then it will be time to expand your vision and allow a new dream to come forth, one that is even bigger than the last one. What is the extent of your true capabilities? You don't know until you test your limits, and I think you'll be surprised when you see all that is possible.

* * *

We started this book together by saying "There is nothing wrong with you—or anyone else." It is my hope that you master Character Coding not only to read a client from across the room, but also to better communicate with people in all areas of your life. Carpe diem, my friends!

Appendix

How to Rock the Character Codes in the Real World

Learning in both business and life is rarely something you check off your list and file away as "done." People who are committed to growing and succeeding recognize that answers point to more questions and success points to new challenges.

In this final section of the book, I have included a number of additional teachings, resources, and even a chance to experience Character Coding in person at Client Success LIVE, a three-day seminar. For some, this marks the end of our journey together; for others, we have only just begun.

The following pages include the 11 Pillars, a complete Master Resource Guide, and bonus tickets. Read through the resources, put them into action, and enjoy!

Brandy

11 Pillars for Your Rock-Solid Platform

In business, you want to be clear about who you are, what you are about, what your message is, whom you serve, and how clients or customers say yes to your product. In fact, I discovered that regardless of the business I was building, or if I wanted to stand out in the corporate environment, there were certain steps to map out and address in order to create success.

When these items were in place, achieving goals was inevitable. These 11 steps were so valuable that I came to refer to them as the 11 Pillars. This same process can be used by anyone—from entrepreneurs who want to create a business based on an idea scribbled on a napkin to the managers or executives planning to launch a product, expand a territory, or rise through the ranks to become a leader in their company.

You have learned all about Character Coding. Now I will show you how I implemented that knowledge using the 11 Pillars. Do you remember from Chapter 2 I mentioned that if you build it, they will come? Well, this is the foundation upon which you will build your strategy as you use the Character Codes. The order of the 11 Pillars isn't random, but carefully created, beginning with knowing yourself and culminating in creating a global perspective as a philanthropist. I recommend that you work them in order and then regularly review as needed.

Pillar 1. Personality

Knowing and showcasing your strengths is key to attracting clients. What makes you uniquely "you" is what sets you apart as a rock star in your company or as a celebrity entrepreneur. You may be thinking, "Of course, I know who I am," and that may be partially true. But how deep have you looked? Are you using this self-knowledge and understanding in your marketing? Most people just focus outward on the client and forget that they are a key asset in their business. People will buy who you are before they buy what you're selling. As you learned Character Coding, you realized we dove deep into all aspects of you—the strengths, the challenges, and the driving need that motivates you. Instead of hiding from it, embrace it and utilize it. Every action we take starts with an idea, feeling, or drive that comes from within. We benefit from being aware of it and serve others with the gifts we bring to the table.

Pillar 2. Purpose

Some in business call this a mission statement, but my definition goes deeper. It is discovering the real *why* behind what you do. I have a seven-step process I guide clients through to get to this answer. The shortcut is to tell you the end result: it is knowing what lesson you want to teach if you have only one message to share with the world. Getting that specific will keep you energized and focused along the journey. This purpose or core message may remain as a personal statement of self, or it may become a marketing message. Either way, it is a driving force that keeps you moving forward and sustains the bridge between you and your clients.

Pillar 3. People

No one is an island, and a business starves without clients. People are the lifeline of your growing business, and so selecting your ideal client is a very important decision. Chapter 8 delved into how the different Character Codes get along and explored successful working relationships. Chapter 9 explained how to attract the clientele you want. Keep in mind that although your ideal clients are important, they don't enter the process until Pillar 3. Note the interconnection between each pillar: figuring out Pillar 1 (you), making Pillar 1 purposeful through Pillar 2 (your why), and utilizing Pillar 2 to reach out with Pillar 3 (your people).

Pillar 4. Potential

This is the big dream, the vision—understanding what your own personal potential is and what is possible in your business. Every great success story teaches that it is essential to have a vision. What the stories often leave out is why. When you are clear about where you want to go, it affects every decision you make today *and* tomorrow.

One decision at a time, day after day, is how you ultimately reach your goal. Without this clarity, you won't be able to make the right decisions when you need to. The good news is you aren't locked into a predetermined plan. You can make adjustments and reevaluate at any time along the way. Spend some time mapping this out, including the main route as well as alternative routes, and use what you learned about the Character Codes to gauge your potential and figure out who can help you reach your goal.

Pillar 5. Passion

What are you really passionate about? What happens for the client as a result of taking this journey with you? What happens when someone buys your product? What does saying yes really mean? If you want to attract clients, you must be able to describe the transformation that comes from working with you. This often isn't the immediate response, but rather the far-reaching consequences. For example, if you sell Widget A that cuts dinner prep time in half, is your message about saving 30 minutes? Or is it a more transformational benefit, what 30 minutes just bought back: more time with kids and your spouse, fewer hassles over daily chores, more time to exercise, feeling less frazzled, etc. This is the Pillar where you focus on what you're really providing and communicate it to your clients. Depending on which Character Code clients you choose to serve, you'll want to make sure this message is delivered in a language they understand.

Pillar 6. Process

I am ultimately a marketer at heart, and I know most marketing experts will tell you never to discuss your process. The process is how you do what you do. It is true that this is dry language and only one of the Character Codes really wants to know this information. However, it is a big seller with *all* the Character Codes to know that you have a process. Clients like to know that you have a system and an organized method behind your work.

Before you discount this Pillar as not relevant for you, please realize that everyone has a process for something. It could be the steps you take in serving your clients, developing or using your product, or organizing your information; or perhaps it's managing your team, treating your patients, or running your events. What I encourage is for you to consciously know and refine your process and possibly even brand it.

Within this Pillar are many strengths and talents you've been taking for granted because they come easily to you. Your unique talents are often why your clients say yes. Knowing how to communicate your process in a very short, understandable way (focusing on the benefits) could help you land the next big account or a promotion or get new clients lining up outside your door.

Pillar 7. Problems

In its most simplistic definition, a business exists to solve a problem for its clients. The problem-solution model is the basis for most inventions, products, and services. Does your back hurt? You need to see a chiropractor. Is your hair greasy? You need to buy shampoo. Did your neighbor sue you? You need to hire an attorney. Are you a rising star surrounded by paparazzi? You need to engage a PR firm. In order to attract clients, you must always be aware of their problems, express understanding or empathy, and then let them know your solution. I have seen business owners who created a great product but were marketing it to the wrong type of clientele, then wonder why no one was buying. Make sure you are solving a problem that your Character Code client needs to have fixed.

Pillar 8. Plan

I do love having a well-laid plan and seeing it executed. Of course, nothing ever goes entirely as planned. There are always many adjustments to make along the way. However, this doesn't mean you should throw out planning! This Pillar is about mapping out and building an organization's or entrepreneur's sales structure. Plan everything precisely: terms, product specs, deliverables, pricing, delivery dates—the works. This Pillar requires a lot of work to complete, but it is worth the effort. I know some Character Codes prefer to wing it and don't want to drill down into specific details, but I encourage you to do it anyway. It is a client turnoff to show up unprepared and hope he or she stills says yes to working with you. True confidence comes when you know you have something rock solid to offer, a competitive price, and a date for delivery. The effort you put into this Pillar will pay you back in dividends.

Pillar 9. Promotion

If you don't promote what you do, you will become the best-kept secret in your industry. This is not a distinction you want to achieve. Most businesses require continuous marketing efforts to ensure a steady stream of clients. Read about driving needs in Chapter 1 again, for it will transform your marketing. Revisit Chapter 10 for more Character Coding in marketing and sales. Knowing which Character Code clients you want to attract, understanding their dreams, fears, and deepest desires, provides invaluable information for your marketing and promotion activities. When it comes to attracting clients, the most important thing to focus on is need. Review the "Psyche" section in each Character Code chapter to make sure you don't waste your time or money pitching to an unwanted need. You want your marketing to pay off and your product or service to be a win-win for everyone involved.

Pillar 10. Progress

This is the Pillar dedicated to tracking the milestones and measurements in your business. It is connected to Pillar 4 in that you first need to know where you are going, and then you use this Pillar to keep tabs on your progress. If you don't pay attention to the details along the way, you won't know if your plan is working—often until it becomes painfully obvious. Milestones and measurements track progress and allow for adjustments and course corrections. Very few plans are executed based on the first draft, and most are revised along the way, so expect to be tweaking as you go along. When it comes to attracting clients, this also means being aware of the needs of the different Character Codes in regard to the *changing* environment, economy, or evolving marketplace factors. Regularly tracking benchmarks in your business is worth the effort. If you are a Class President or Scholar Character Code, this sounds logical and you are ready to go. Some of the other Character Codes dread this Pillar. Not everyone needs to use a spreadsheet to track the details, but at a minimum, you need awareness and a plan in order to reach your goal.

Pillar 11. Philanthropy

In the beginning, you may be motivated simply by basic survival needs. Over time, you may become intensely interested in multiplying your product or service message. Then you will likely wish to expand your business and improve your overall quality of life. Ultimately though, you will want to have a bigger view for your business and yourself. Interestingly, your clients will love having something more to get behind when they buy your product or service.

This Pillar is about making what you do and sell bigger than just you. You will want to give back to keep the cycle of abundance and success flowing. This is a Pillar you can put into action even in the beginning of a new business or venture. Adding this Pillar to your portfolio causes a shift in your thinking, from simple survival to a more global mindset as a caring philanthropist. Choose your philanthropy based on what matters to you, and it is likely to resonate with your Character Code clients. This Pillar is a win-win-win, elevating you as a business owner, attracting clients, and serving your chosen community through the philanthropy.

Master Resource Guide—
How to Read a Client Now

Additional resources, downloads, quizzes, slides, and videos were listed at the end of each chapter. Here is a complete list and the links to access them, including a few new ones you'll want to check out.

Chapter 1. The Creation of the Character Code System

» Take the online shortcut quiz "Which Character Code Are You?" at http://charactercode.com/quiz. It will shed light on why you do what you do and will take you less than five minutes to complete.

» Download the resource "Driving Needs for Each Character Code and How to Keep Your Clients Happy" at http://charactercode.com/happyclients.

» Access the "Character Codes at a Glance" chart in color at http://charactercode.com/ataglance.

Chapter 2. The Challenges We Face in Attracting Clients

» Download the resource "Deal Maker—Where to Focus in the First Impression" at http://charactercode.com/firstimpression.

» Access the "Assumptions in Action" to visually see the assumptions via pictures. Make your own judgment call at http://charactercode.com/assumptions.

Chapter 3. The Class President Character Code

» Download the "Class President Character Code Overview" to have the details and color sketches right at your fingertips at http://charactercode.com/classpresident.

» Access the resource "Taming the Class President Meanie" for tips and insight (and a little humor) at http://charactercode .com/classpresidentmeanie.

Chapter 4. The Cheerleader Character Code

» Download the "Cheerleader Character Code Overview" to have the details and color sketches right at your fingertips at http://charactercode.com/cheerleader.

» Access the resource "Taming the Cheerleader Meanie" for tips and insight (and a little humor) at http://charactercode .com/cheerleadermeanie.

Chapter 5. The Actor Character Code

» Download the "Actor Character Code Overview" to have the details and color sketches right at your fingertips at http:// charactercode.com/actor.

» Access the resource "Taming the Actor Meanie" for tips and insight (and a little humor) at http://charactercode.com/ actormeanie.

Chapter 6. The Scholar Character Code

» Download the "Scholar Character Code Overview" to have the details and color sketches right at your fingertips at http:// charactercode.com/scholar.

» Access the resource "Taming the Scholar Meanie" for tips and insight (and a little humor) at http://charactercode.com/ scholarmeanie.

Chapter 7. The Activist Character Code

» Download the "Activist Character Code Overview" to have the details and color sketches right at your fingertips at http:// charactercode.com/activist.

» Access the resource "Taming the Activist Meanie" for tips and insight (and a little humor) at http://charactercode.com/activistmeanie.

Chapter 8. The Artist Character Code

» Download the "Artist Character Code Overview" to have the details and color sketches right at your fingertips at http://charactercode.com/artist.

» Access the resource "Taming the Artist Meanie" for tips and insight (and a little humor) at http://charactercode.com/artistmeanie.

Chapter 9. Which Character Codes Get Along and Which Clash?

» Download the resource "Shortcut to the Best Character Code Matchups" at http://charactercode.com/matchup.

» Access the "Character Codes Combos" chart in color at http://charactercode.com/combos.

Chapter 10. The Character Codes in Marketing and Sales

» Access the "Think Fast—Shortcut to Character Coding" pairing chart and resource guide at http://charactercode.com/thinkfast.

» Download the expanded resource "Client Attraction Turnoff's and Turn-on's" at http://charactercode.com/clientattraction.

» Access the "How to Work a Room" resource and stories to learn more about using Character Coding in your networking at http://charactercode.com/workaroom.

Chapter 11. Putting the Character Codes in Action

» Access the "Heroic Journey" resource and stories to learn more about using Character Coding to make things happen at http://charactercode.com/heroicjourney.

Additional Resources

» Submit your "Character Coding Story" for possible publication and share your Character Code stories at http://charactercode.com/story.

» Put Character Coding into action at the Brandy Mychals' Client Success LIVE seminar and claim your two VIP bonus tickets for free ($1,500 savings) at http://charactercode.com.

Notes

Chapter 2

1. J. Pfeffer, "Shape Perceptions of Your Work, Early and Often," *Harvard Business Review*, October 21, 2010.

2. A. Mehrabian, *Silent Messages: Implicit Communication of Emotions and Attitudes*, Belmont, CA: Wadsworth, 1981.

3. Mehrabian, *Silent Messages*.

4. Mehrabian, *Silent Messages*.

5. M. Gladwell, *Blink*, Boston: Little Brown, 2005.

6. A. Chintalapati, H. Sheng, R. Hall, and R. Landers, "Evaluation of Rapid Development System Using Eye Tracker," in *Proceedings of the 2010 American Society for Engineering Education Annual Conference (ASEE)*, Louisville, KY, June 20, 2010.

7. R. Ailes, *You Are the Message*, New York: Crown Business, 1989.

8. S. S. Chun et al., "Unconscious Determinants of Free Decisions in the Human Brain," *Nature Neuroscience*, April 13, 2008.

Chapter 10

1. D. Goleman, "Social Anxiety: New Focus Leads to Insights and Therapy," *New York Times*, 1984.

Acknowledgments

I'm grateful for the support from my family, friends, and clients who have encouraged me to write this book. I celebrate the thousands of people that have put the Character Code System in daily use through relationships in work and play.

A huge thank you to Phyllis Parsons, Dana Newman, Brandy Rivers, Sandra Yancey, Vinca Heart, John Heart, Lisa Ferrer, and Michael Potter for believing in me and sharing your talents to make this all possible. They were all there at important points in the journey that led to this book, encouraging me and cheering me on.

It is with gratitude that I acknowledge the decades of professors and trainers that crossed my path. I would run out of paper if I listed them all, from every discipline I have studied to the degrees I earned, to the business and motivational trainings I attended. It has been a lifetime of learning, and I look forward to keeping this questioning and observing nature alive, as that's what led me to create the Character Codes.

To the many friends and clients that said yes and helped me share this system with the world, you are a big part of this success. I celebrate you and appreciate you! A big hug to all the assistants and volunteers who held the space at the many workshops and events that first introduced Character Codes to the world.

Thank you to McGraw-Hill senior editor Donya Dickerson and the entire staff that grabbed hold of this book and ran with it. You broke all the rules we hear about global publishing for first-time authors and the time it takes to bring a book to market. I love our partnership and the way you have embraced Character Coding!

I'm also grateful (this may surprise you) for the many challenges and frustrations I faced along the way. Without the battles, miscommunications, and feelings of being lost, there wouldn't have been a need to create a system to be "found." I celebrate the struggles that caused me to pay closer attention to the world and the people around me and to recognize how we behave and what we really need.

The ultimate gratitude and biggest mommy hug goes to my daughter, Bella. She motivates and inspires me every day. Raising a child who understands the Character Codes will keep you on your toes. She is a gift to me and the world.

And finally, I thank the readers who are the biggest testament to Character Coding, as you put this into action to create the life you desire.

Index

About the Author

Brandy Mychals is a communications expert, sought-after speaker, and the creator of the Character Code System. She's the winner of the 2011 International FEMTOR Award presented by eWomenNetwork.

Having graduated from the Honors College at Loyola Marymount University in communications, Brandy continued her studies and graduated with a doctorate of chiropractic. After having built a successful business and creating an investment portfolio, she suffered a debilitating car accident.

Brandy was diagnosed with a permanent brain injury that left her unable to read for seven years. In this time she went through a divorce, was embroiled in legal battles that left her with no money, and teetered on the brink of bankruptcy.

While going through this life-altering experience as a single mom, she fought back, healed, and wrote and created her Character Code System. Within the first year of launching her new business, she created over $300,000 in sales.

Brandy broke all the publishing rules with *How to Read a Client from Across the Room: Win More Business with the Proven Character Code System*, published by McGraw-Hill. Her proposal was picked up within just two weeks of hitting the streets, and the book was published within eight months of the signed contract. Brandy knows how to create success fast!

You can see Brandy in any of her multiple-media appearances, but the best way is to see her live in action. Her training events have inspired thousands of people to become more confident, improve their communication skills, and attract the right clients. Visit her and get the latest Character Code tips at www.brandymychals.com.

SPECIAL BONUS FOR OUR READERS

Brandy Mychals's Three-Day Seminar Intensive for FREE!

Put the Character Code System and Brandy's Business Training into Action at Client Success LIVE

As a thank you gift for buying *How to Read a Client from Across the Room*, Brandy Mychals is offering a scholarship ticket for you and a friend to her exclusive three-day Client Success LIVE seminar. You will attend as her guests, plus be welcomed by Brandy personally during a private meet and greet just for VIPs. That is a value of $1,500 for free!

Save your seat at www.charactercode.com immediately, as space is limited. This offer is made on a space-available basis and only to those that purchase *How to Read a Client from Across the Room*, published by McGraw-Hill. Any updates will be listed on the website.

Attend the Client Success LIVE weekend intensive seminar to expand upon the insights provided by this book, including:

>> How to apply the Character Codes to your everyday life and business

>> Little-known secrets that will turn you into a networking genius at every event

>> Money mindset and leveraged thinking that they don't teach in school

>> A step-by-step process to master any goal you desire for a life free of regrets

>> The 10 principles to creating balance in work, life, and love

- » Rarely revealed money blocks affecting you and your clients
- » What it really takes to make things happen and how to start right away

By the end of the weekend, you'll be ready to make your own heroic journey and create the success you desire.

As the "Queen of Content," Brandy shares more than just motivational stories. She is known for her marketing and sales systems, branding brilliance, and the leadership skills she used to create her own business. Her specialty is telling the behind-the-scenes secrets to making things happen—fast. Brandy says, "Now it is your turn!"

If you are an entrepreneur or an executive or are wondering which direction to take, this is the weekend for you. If you aren't living the life of your dreams, have achieved success but recently plateaued, or just know there is something more that life has to offer you, then register for Client Success LIVE today. Whether you want to launch a million-dollar idea, rise through the corporate ranks, or find the happiness in business and life you've been looking for, this course will change you. Register now at www.charactercode.com.